Kaplan Publishing are constan
ways to make a difference to y(
exciting online resources really
different to students looking fo. ∪∧∪⁻ success.

GW01090699

This book comes with free MyKaplan online resources so that you can study anytime, anywhere. This free online resource is not sold separately and is included in the price of the book.

Having purchased this book, you have access to the following online study materials:

CONTENT	ACCA (including FFA,FAB,FMA)		FIA (excluding FFA,FAB,FMA)	
	Text	Kit	Text	Kit
Eletronic version of the book	✓	✓	✓	✓
Check Your Understanding Test with instant answers	✓			
Material updates	✓	✓	✓	✓
Latest official ACCA exam questions*		✓		
Extra question assistance using the signpost icon**		✓		
Question debriefs using clock icon***		✓		
Consolidation Test including questions and answers	✓			

*   Excludes AB, MA, FA, LW, FAB, FMA and FFA; for all other subjects includes a selection of questions, as released by ACCA
**   For ACCA SBR, AFM, APM, AAA only
*** Excludes AB, MA, FA, LW, FAB, FMA and FFA

How to access your online resources

Kaplan Financial students will already have a MyKaplan account and these extra resources will be available to you online. You do not need to register again, as this process was completed when you enrolled. If you are having problems accessing online materials, please ask your course administrator.

If you are not studying with Kaplan and did not purchase your book via a Kaplan website, to unlock your extra online resources please go to www.mykaplan.co.uk/addabook (even if you have set up an account and registered books previously). You will then need to enter the ISBN number (on the title page and back cover) and the unique pass key number contained in the scratch panel below to gain access.

You will also be required to enter additional information during this process to set up or confirm your account details.

If you purchased through Kaplan Flexible Learning or via the Kaplan Publishing website you will automatically receive an e-mail invitation to MyKaplan. Please register your details using this email to gain access to your content. If you do not receive the e-mail or book content, please contact Kaplan Publishing.

Your Code and Information

This code can only be used once for the registration of one book online. This registration and your online content will expire when the final sittings for the examinations covered by this book have taken place. Please allow one hour from the time you submit your book details for us to process your request.

Please scratch the film to access your MyKaplan code.

Please be aware that this code is case-sensitive and you will need to include the dashes within the passcode, but not when entering the ISBN. For further technical support, please visit www.MyKaplan.co.uk

INTERMEDIATE CERTIFICATE

FA2

Maintaining Financial Records

EXAM KIT

British Library Cataloguing-in-Publication Data

A catalogue record for this book is available from the British Library.

Published by Kaplan Publishing UK

Unit 2 The Business Centre

Molly Millar's Lane

Wokingham

Berkshire

RG41 2QZ

ISBN: 978-1-78740-336-9

Acknowledgements

These materials are reviewed by the ACCA examining team. The objective of the review is to ensure that the material properly covers the syllabus and study guide outcomes, used by the examining team in setting the exams, in the appropriate breadth and depth. The review does not ensure that every eventuality, combination or application of examinable topics is addressed by the ACCA Approved Content. Nor does the review comprise a detailed technical check of the content as the Approved Content Provider has its own quality assurance processes in place in this respect.

This product contains material that is ©Financial Reporting Council Ltd (FRC). Adapted and reproduced with the kind permission of the Financial Reporting Council. All rights reserved. For further information, please visit www.frc.org.uk or call +44 (0)20 7492 2300.

We are grateful to the Association of Chartered Certified Accountants for the permission to reproduce past examination questions. The answers have been prepared by Kaplan Publishing.

INTRODUCTION

Packed with questions, this book will help you to successfully prepare for your examination.

- All questions are grouped by syllabus topics.
- Objective test questions are of exam standard and format – this enables you to master the examination techniques.

The exam kit begins with some short revision questions to ensure you will get the most from the exam standard questions when you attempt them. Start by attempting the revision questions. Marks are given as an indication of the difficulty of the question.

When you have completed section 1, revision questions, and you have revised any areas of difficulty as highlighted by this exercise, you may attempt section 2 comprising objective test questions.

For further information about the FA2 examination please refer to ACCA website:

www.accaglobal.com

ENHANCEMENTS

We have added the following enhancement to the answers in this exam kit:

Tutorial note

Some answers include tutorial notes to explain some of the technical points in more detail.

CONTENTS

Section

Quality and accuracy are of the utmost importance to us so if you spot an error in any of our products, please send an email to mykaplanreporting@kaplan.com with full details.

Our Quality Co-ordinator will work with our technical team to verify the error and take action to ensure it is corrected in future editions.

KAPLAN PUBLISHING

INDEX TO QUESTIONS AND ANSWERS

SYLLABUS AND REVISION GUIDANCE

SYLLABUS CONTENT

FA2 *Maintaining Financial Records* introduces the fundamental principles of accounting and develops the knowledge and understanding required to maintain accounting records. You will learn to produce accounting records, extract a trial balance and make necessary adjustments to produce an extended trial balance and basic financial statements. The syllabus covers accounting for the business transactions of sole traders and partnerships.

A   GENERALLY ACCEPTED ACCOUNTING PRINCIPLES AND CONCEPTS

1   The key accounting principles and characteristics

(a)   Explain the accounting principles of accounting.

   (i)   Going concern

   (ii)   Accruals

   (iii)   Consistency

   (iv)   Double entry

   (v)   Business entity

   (vi)   Materiality

   (vii)   Historical cost

(b)   Explain the qualitative accounting characteristics relating to.

   (i)   Relevance

   (ii)   Faithful representation

   (iii)   Comparability

   (iv)   Verifiability

   (v)   Timeliness

   (vi)   Understandability

2   Maintaining financial records

(a)   Explain the importance of maintaining financial records for internal and external use.

(b)   Describe the type of accounting records that a business should maintain and the main uses of each.

3   The regulatory framework

(a)   Describe the main requirements of accounting standards in relation to syllabus area D.

B   THE PRINCIPLES AND PROCESS OF BASIC BOOKKEEPING

1   The elements of the financial statements

(a)   Explain the meaning of the accounting equation.

(b)   Describe the meaning of assets, liabilities and capital in an accounting context.

(c)   Describe the components of a set of final accounts for a sole trader.

2   Books of prime entry and the flow of accounting information in the production of financial statements

(a)   Explain the purpose and use of books of prime entry and ledger accounts.

(b)   Identify reasons for closing off accounts and producing a trial balance.

(c)   Explain the process of preparing a set of final accounts from a trial balance.

C   THE PREPARATION OF JOURNALS AND LEDGER ACCOUNTS

1   Preparation of journals from the books of prime entry

(a)   Explain and illustrate the dual aspect convention.

(b)   Prepare journals to record transactions in an appropriate format.

2   Preparation of ledger accounts

(a)   Explain the purpose and use of ledger accounts.

(b)   Post journals and other entries into the appropriate ledger account.

(c)   Balance the ledger accounts carrying down and bringing down balances as appropriate.

D   RECORDING TRANSACTIONS AND EVENTS

1   Sales and purchases

(a)   Record sale and purchases transactions in ledger accounts.

(b)   Record sales and purchase returns.

(c)   Account for trade and settlement discounts.

(d)   Identify sources of information on sales tax and explain the relationship between the entity and the relevant government agency.

(e)   Explain the general principles of the operation of a sales tax including:

   (i)   requirements for registration

   (ii)   main information to be included on business documentation

   (iii)   types of taxable supplies and their classification for sales tax

   (iv)   accounting and payment of sales tax

   (v)   penalties for late returns or late payment sales tax.

(f)   Explain the different methods of accounting and reporting for sales tax.

(g)   Identify and obtain sales tax data from the accounting system.

(h)   Calculate sales tax on inputs and outputs.

(i)   Record the consequent accounting entries and calculate the sales tax due to/from the business.

(j)   Compute the main components of a sales tax return.

(k)   Communicate effectively with the relevant tax authority about sales tax matters including potential adjustments, errors or omissions.

(l)   Calculate the cash flow impact on the business of the payment of sales tax and the potential impact on the business of any changes in legislation for sales tax.

2   Cash and bank

(a)   Record cash and bank transactions in ledger accounts.

(b)   Report cash and bank balances in the final accounts.

3   Inventory

(a)   Recognise the need for adjustments for inventory in preparing financial statements.

(b)   Record opening and closing inventory.

(c)   Identify and apply the alternative methods of valuing inventory.

(d)   Explain and apply the IASB requirements for valuing inventories.

(e)   Recognise which costs should be included when valuing inventories.

(f)   Explain the use of continuous and period end inventory records.

(g)   Calculate the value of closing inventory using FIFO (first in, first out) and AVCO (average cost) both periodic weighted average and continuous weighted average.

(h)   Identify the impact of inventory valuation methods on profit, assets and capital including:

(i)   periodic weighted average

(ii)   continuous weighted average

(iii) FIFO.

(i)   Report inventory in the final accounts.

4   Tangible non-current assets and depreciation

(a)   Define non-current assets.

(b)   Recognise the difference between current and non-current assets.

(c)   Explain the difference between capital and revenue items.

(d)   Classify expenditure as capital or revenue expenditure.

(e)   Explain the impact of misclassification of capital expenditure as revenue expenditure and vice versa on the statement of profit or loss and the statement of financial position.

(f)   Prepare journal and ledger entries to record the acquisition and disposal of non-current assets (including part exchange).

(g) Calculate and record profits or losses on disposal of non-current assets in the statement of profit or loss including part exchange transactions and scrapping of assets.

(h) Explain the purpose of depreciation.

(i) Calculate the charge for depreciation using straight line and reducing balance methods.

(j) Identify the circumstances where different methods of calculating depreciation would be appropriate.

(k) Illustrate how depreciation expense and accumulated depreciation are recorded in ledger accounts.

(l) Explain the purpose and function of an asset register.

(m) Prepare the non-current asset register accounting for all or part of the following:

   (i) acquisition including authorisation

   (ii) part exchange and cash non-current asset purchases

   (iii) depreciation.

(n) Identify and resolve any discrepancies relating to the accounting records for non-current assets.

(o) Report non-current assets and depreciation in the final accounts.

5 Accruals and prepayments

(a) Apply the matching concept applies to accruals and prepayments.

(b) Identify and calculate the adjustments needed for accruals and prepayments in preparing financial statements.

(c) Illustrate the process of adjusting for accruals and prepayments in preparing final accounts.

(d) Prepare the journal entries and ledger entries for the creation of an accrual or prepayment.

(e) Identify the impact on profit, net assets and capital of accruals and prepayments.

(f) Report accruals and prepayments in the final accounts.

6 Receivables, payables and provisions

(a) Explain and identify examples of receivables and payables.

(b) Prepare the bookkeeping entries to write off an irrecoverable debt.

(c) Record an irrecoverable debt recovered.

(d) Identify the impact of irrecoverable debts on the statement of profit or loss and on the statement of financial position.

(e) Calculate the movement in the allowance for receivables and the closing balance.

(f) Prepare the bookkeeping entries to create and adjust an allowance for receivables.

(g) Illustrate how to include movements in the allowance for receivables in the statement of profit or loss and how the closing balance of the allowance should be reported in the statement of financial position.

(h) Account for contras between trade receivables and payables.

(i) Explain the nature of provisions and liabilities.

(j) Distinguish between a provision and liability.

(k) Account for provisions and liabilities.

(l) Report provisions and liabilities in the final accounts.

7 Capital and finance costs

(a) Distinguish between capital injected by the business owner(s) and third parties for an unincorporated business.

(b) Explain the accounting equation including the impact of changes in capital.

(c) Prepare the capital ledger account for an unincorporated business.

E PREPARING A TRIAL BALANCE AND ERRORS

1 Trial balance

(a) Explain the purpose of the trial balance.

(b) Distinguish between errors which will be detected by extracting a trial balance and those which will not.

(c) Calculate and explain the impact of errors on the statement of profit or loss and the statement of financial position.

(d) Identify the limitations of the trial balance.

(e) Prepare the initial trial balance.

2 Correction of errors

(a) Explain the purpose of, and reasons for, creating a suspense account

(b) Identify different types of bookkeeping error including those that result in suspense accounts.

(c) Identify and explain the action required to correct errors including clearing any suspense accounts.

(d) Prepare correcting journal entries.

(e) Record correcting entries in the ledgers.

(f) Demonstrate how the final accounts are affected by the correction of errors.

F RECONCILIATIONS

1 Control account reconciliations

(a) Explain the purpose of reconciliation of the receivables and payables ledger control accounts.

(b) Identify errors in the ledger control accounts and list of balances.

(c) Make correcting entries in the ledger control accounts.

(d) Prepare a reconciliation between the list of balances and the corrected ledger control accounts.

(e) Identify the control account balance to be reported in the final accounts.

(f) Prepare a reconciliation of a supplier's statement and the supplier's account in the payables ledger.

2 Bank reconciliation

(a) Explain the purpose of reconciliation of the bank ledger account to the corresponding bank statement.

(b) Identify errors and omissions in the bank ledger account and bank statement.

(c) Identify timing differences.

(d) Make the correcting entries in the bank ledger account.

(e) Prepare the reconciliation between the bank statement balance and the corrected bank ledger account.

(f) Identify the bank balance to be reported in the final accounts.

G THE TRIAL BALANCE AND THE EXTENDED TRIAL BALANCE

1 Preparation of the trial balance/extended trial balance

(a) Explain the process of extending the trial balance.

(b) Record the correction of errors on the extended trial balance.

(c) Explain and record post trial balance adjustments on the extended trial balance:

    (i) Accruals and prepayments

    (ii) Depreciation

    (iii) Provisions

    (iv) Closing inventory

    (v) Allowance for receivables

    (vi) Irrecoverable debts

    (vii) Non-current asset transactions.

(d) Extend and complete the extended trial balance including calculating the final reported profit or loss.

(e) Prepare the opening trial balance for the next accounting period.

2   Preparation of the final accounts including incomplete records

(a)   Explain the process of preparing a set of final accounts from a trial balance.

(b)   Explain the format and purpose of the statement of profit or loss and statement of financial position for a sole trader.

(c)   Prepare the final accounts for a sole trader from:

(i)   The extended trial balance or

(ii)   Directly from ledger accounts or

(iii)   Trial balance.

(d)   Describe the circumstances which lead to incomplete records.

(e)   Describe the methods of constructing accounts from incomplete records.

(f)   Prepare the final accounts or elements thereof using incomplete record techniques such as:

(i)   Mark ups and margins

(ii)   Ledger accounts to derive missing figures

(iii)   Manipulation of the accounting equation.

H   PARTNERSHIPS

1   Partnership agreement

(a)   Define a partnership.

(b)   Explain the purpose and content of a partnership agreement.

(c)   Explain, calculate and account for appropriations of profit:

(i)   Salaries of partners

(ii)   Interest on drawings

(iii)   Interest on capital

(iv)   Share of residual profit (the amount of profit available to be shared between the partners in the profit and loss sharing ratio, after all other appropriations have been made).

2   Partnership accounting records

(a)   Explain the difference between partners' capital and current accounts.

(b)   Prepare the partners' capital and current accounts.

3   Partnership financial statements and change in partnership

(a)   Prepare the final accounts for a partnership.

(b)   Explain and account for the admission of a new partner including the treatment of any goodwill arising.

Note: Candidates will not be expected to calculate the value of goodwill.

PLANNING YOUR REVISION

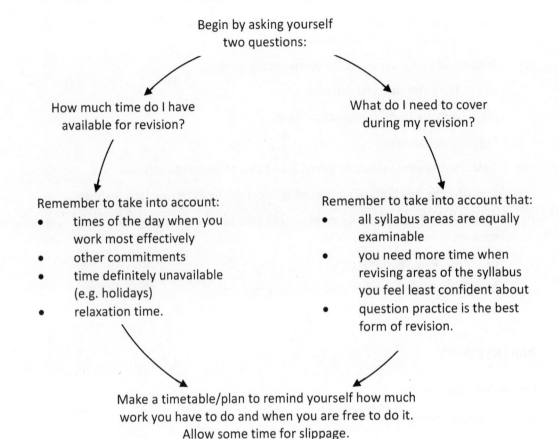

Begin by asking yourself
two questions:

How much time do I have
available for revision?

What do I need to cover
during my revision?

Remember to take into account:
- times of the day when you work most effectively
- other commitments
- time definitely unavailable (e.g. holidays)
- relaxation time.

Remember to take into account that:
- all syllabus areas are equally examinable
- you need more time when revising areas of the syllabus you feel least confident about
- question practice is the best form of revision.

Make a timetable/plan to remind yourself how much
work you have to do and when you are free to do it.
Allow some time for slippage.

REVISION TECHNIQUES

- Go through your notes and textbook highlighting the important points.
- You might want to produce your own set of **summarised notes.**
- **List key words** for each topic to remind you of the essential concepts.
- **Practise exam-standard questions**, under timed conditions.
- **Rework questions** that you got completely wrong the first time, but only when you think you know the subject better.
- If you get stuck on topics, **find someone to explain** them to you (your tutor or a colleague, for example).
- **Read recent articles** on the ACCA website or in the student magazine.
- **Read** good newspapers and professional journals.

THE EXAMINATION

FORMAT OF THE EXAM

The format of the computer-based exam is as follows:

Total time allowed: 2 hours.

	Number of marks
50 compulsory objective test questions (2 marks each)	100
	————

Answering the questions

- **Objective test questions** – read the questions carefully and work through any calculations required. If you have a choice of answers and don't know the answer, then guess.

- **Data entry questions** – ensure that you attempt all questions – if necessary try to do the calculations, even if you are unsure.

- **If you get stuck with a question** skip it and return to it later.

- **Answer every question** – if you do not know the answer, you do not lose anything by guessing. Towards the end of the examination spend the last five minutes reading through your answers and making any corrections.

- **Equally divide the time** you spend on questions. In a two-hour examination that has 50 questions you have about 2.4 minutes per a question.

- **Do not skip any part of the syllabus** and make sure that you have *learnt* definitions, *know* key words and their meanings and importance, and *understand* the names and meanings of rules, concepts and theories.

- Bear in mind that this exam includes both narrative and computational questions, so ensure that you are able to deal with both types of question.

Computer-based examinations

- Be sure you understand how to use the **software** before you start the exam. If in doubt, ask the assessment centre staff to explain it to you.

- Questions are **displayed on the screen** and answers are entered using keyboard and mouse. At the end of the exam, you are given a certificate showing the result you have achieved.

- **Don't panic** if you realise you've answered a question incorrectly – you can always go back and change your answer.

- The CBE question types are as follows:

  - Multiple choice – where you are required to choose one answer from a list of options provided by clicking on the appropriate 'radio button'

  - Multiple response – where you are required to select more than one response from the options provided by clicking on the appropriate tick boxes(typically choose two options from the available list

  - Multiple response matching – where you are required to indicate a response to a number of related statements by clicking on the 'radio button' which corresponds to the appropriate response for each statement

  - Number entry – where you are required to key in a response to a question shown on the screen.

Section 1

REVISION QUESTIONS

ACCOUNTING PRINCIPLES AND CONCEPTS

1   State two ways in which accounting standards (IASs and IFRSs) improve financial accounting. **(3 marks)**

2   Briefly explain the going concern concept. **(2 marks)**

3   The *Conceptual Framework for Financial Reporting* states that in order to be useful, financial information should have the following fundamental and enhancing qualitative characteristics:

   (i)   relevance

   (ii)   faithful representation

   (iii)   comparability

   (iv)   verifiability

   (v)   timelines, and

   (vi)   understandability.

   Briefly explain any two of these qualitative characteristics. **(4 marks)**

4   Briefly explain the business entity concept and its impact on the recording of transactions. **(2 marks)**

5   Explain why every transaction is recorded using both a debit entry and a credit entry. **(3 marks)**

BASIC BOOKKEEPING

6   Define the terms 'asset' and 'liability', and provide one example of each.   **(4 marks)**

7   Explain how each element of the accounting equation is affected when goods for resale are purchased on credit.   **(3 marks)**

8   Explain how settlement discounts should be treated when an entity is raising a sales invoice and the customer is not expected to take advantage of the early settlement discount offered.   **(3 marks)**

9   Explain how settlement discounts should be treated when an entity is raising a sales invoice and the customer is expected to take advantage of the early settlement discount offered.   **(3 marks)**

NON-CURRENT ASSETS AND DEPRECIATION

10   Give three reasons why there may be a difference between the assets listed on the non-current asset register and the physical presence of assets.   **(3 marks)**

11   Your friend, a self-employed motor mechanic, has recently disposed of an old set of ramps from his garage. He is unsure how he can calculate whether he has made a profit or loss on the disposal of this asset.

Briefly explain to him what factors he would need to account for in calculating the profit or loss on sale.   **(4 marks)**

12   Calculate the annual depreciation charge for five years, for a non-current asset costing $15,000, to be depreciated at a rate of 25% using the reducing balance method.   **(4 marks)**

CONTROL ACCOUNTS, RECONCILIATIONS AND ERRORS

13   You are helping a friend, a self-employed hairdresser, with her financial record keeping. You notice that she has posted the purchase of a new set of adjustable chairs for the salon to the repairs account. You bring this error to her attention.

Briefly explain what type of error this is and why it is important to correct this posting in the accounts.   **(3 marks)**

14   A friend of yours in business as an hotelier says whenever she receives a bank statement the balance rarely agrees with that shown in her cash book.

Briefly explain the reason for such differences.   **(3 marks)**

15   State and explain two reasons for maintaining control accounts.   **(4 marks)**

ADJUSTMENTS TO THE TRIAL BALANCE

16   Explain the main purpose of a trial balance.   **(2 marks)**

17   Briefly explain the differences between an irrecoverable debt and an allowance for receivables and the accounting treatment of each.   **(4 marks)**

18   The inventory sheet of a business retailing children's clothes showed a batch of summer t-shirts at a cost of $300. It seems clear that these will be later included in a sale and will be expected to realise $180.

Briefly explain at what value the t-shirts should be correctly shown in the inventory valuation and what principle it is based upon.   **(2 marks)**

19   A friend of yours has recently received her first set of financial accounts from her accountant for her first year of trading. She says she does not understand why on the statement of financial position there are terms like accruals and prepayments.

Explain which accounting concept has been applied here and the purpose of this principle when drafting first accounts.   **(3 marks)**

FINAL ACCOUNTS

20   State the purpose of:

(i)   the statement of profit or loss; and

(ii)   the statement of financial position.   **(2 marks)**

21   A significant difference between the statement of financial position of a sole trader and that of a partnership is that a partnership's statement of financial position includes the partners' current accounts.

Explain what entries are made to a partner's current account and what a closing credit balance would represent.   **(2 marks)**

22   What are the main contents of a partnership agreement?   **(2 marks)**

23   State the five steps that should be followed when determining when, and how much, revenue should be recognised in the financial statements.   **(3 marks)**

Section 2

OBJECTIVE TEST QUESTIONS

ACCOUNTING PRINCIPLES AND CONCEPTS

1   Which accounting principle is described by the following statement?

'It is a threshold quality that requires information is disclosed if it is likely to affect decisions made by users of financial statements.'

A   Prudence

B   Materiality

C   Going concern

D   Business entity

2   Which of the following statements best explains the importance of maintaining financial records?

A   Financial records should be maintained for the sole purpose of enabling the business owner to make management and control decisions.

B   Financial records should be maintained for the sole purpose of enabling the business owner to make information available to external interested parties.

C   Financial records should be maintained for the sole purpose of enabling the business owner to determine any tax liability arising.

D   Financial records should be maintained to enable a business owner to make decisions regarding the business and to make information available to interested external parties when appropriate to do so.

3   Which of the following are fundamental qualitative characteristics of financial information according to the *Conceptual Framework for Financial Reporting*?

(i)   Relevance

(ii)   Reliability

A   (i) and (ii)

B   (i) only

C   Neither (i) nor (ii)

D   (ii) only

4   The principle of consistency is best described by which of the following statements?

A   Transaction should be accounted for on a consistent basis within an accounting period only.

B   Transactions should be accounted for on a consistent basis from one accounting period to another.

C   Transactions relating to the statement of financial position only should be accounted for on a consistent basis.

D   Transactions should be accounted for on a consistent basis, both within an accounting period, and from one accounting period to another.

5   Which accounting principle is described by the following statement?

'For accounting purposes, a business is separate from its owners.'

A   Going concern

B   Materiality

C   Business entity

D   Prudence

6   The *Conceptual Framework for Financial Reporting* includes guidance on how assets and liabilities should be classified in the financial statements.

How should each of the following items be classified for inclusion in the financial statements?

	Statement of profit or loss	Statement of financial position
Expenses	✓	
Equity		✓

7   **How should each of the following items be classified according to the *Conceptual Framework for Financial Reporting*?**

	Fundamental qualitative characteristic	Enhancing qualitative characteristic
Understandability		✓
Faithful representation	✓	

8   Which TWO of the following are enhancing qualitative characteristics of financial information according to the *Conceptual Framework for Financial Reporting*?

	Selected answer
Going concern	
Comparability	✓
Timeliness	✓
Relevance	

9   Which TWO of the following are enhancing qualitative characteristics of financial information according to the *Conceptual Framework for Financial Reporting*?

	Selected answer
Verifiability	✓
Materiality	
Historical cost	
Understandability	✓

10   Which TWO of the following are fundamental qualitative characteristics of financial information according to the *Conceptual Framework for Financial Reporting*?

	Selected answer
Relevance	✓
Reliability	
Faithful representation	✓
Verifiability	

11   Which of the following statements best explains the going concern principle?

A   The business is not expected to continue operating for the foreseeable future.

B   There is a reasonable expectation that the business will continue operating for the foreseeable future.

C   It is guaranteed that the business will continue operating for the foreseeable future.

D   The business will terminate its operating activities within the foreseeable future.

12   Which of the following statements best explains the historical cost principle?

A   It is represented by the cost of an asset when it was purchased

B   It is represented by the cost of replacing an asset

C   It is represented by the current market value of an asset

D   It is represented by net realisable value of an asset

13 A business includes in the valuation of its closing inventory some goods that were received before the year end, but for which invoices were not received until after the year end.

Which accounting concept is this in accordance with?

A   the historical cost concept

B   the accruals concept

C   the consistency concept

D   the materiality concept

14 **Which of the following statements is NOT true in relation to the importance of a proprietor maintaining financial records for internal use?**

A   Accounting records enable the proprietor to manage and control the business

B   Accounting records enable the proprietor to reconcile the bank and cash balances

C   Accounting records enable the proprietor to make investment decisions regarding the business

D   Accounting records enable the proprietor to provide information that may be of interest to the general public

15 **Which of the following statements is NOT true in relation to the importance of a proprietor maintaining financial records for external use?**

A   They enable the proprietor to provide information to lenders and creditors of the business to support credit and loan applications.

B   They enable the proprietor to make investment decisions relating to the business.

C   They enable the proprietor to provide information to the tax authorities relevant to the business.

D   They enable interested parties, such as the general public, to review and evaluate the financial and economic impact that the business has upon the community.

16 **What is the purpose of a credit note?**

A   It acknowledges a purchase on credit.

B   It is a reference from an agency detailing the creditworthiness of a new customer.

C   It is issued when a deposit is paid on goods.

D   It is issued to cancel all or part of a sales invoice.

17 **Which THREE items below identify the purpose of a purchase invoice?**

	Selected answer
To claim back the sales tax	✓
To identify the goods bought	✓
To record how much is owed to the supplier	✓
To record how much is owed from the customer	

18   Keith received a document from Cullen's Stationery Supplies for eight reams of paper which had been supplied three previously. How should Keith refer to this document?

   A   It is a goods received note

   B   It is a receipt

   C   It is a purchase invoice

   D   It is a credit note

19   Why must a business retain documents?

   A   Because it has always been done

   B   For historical purposes

   C   It is a requirement of tax law

   D   To facilitate planning

PRINCIPLES AND PROCESSES OF BASIC BOOKKEEPING

20   Which of the following statements best describes current assets?

   A   Assets which are currently located on the business premises

   B   Assets which are used to conduct the organisation's current business

   C   Assets which are expected to be converted into cash in the short term

   D   Assets which are not expected to be converted into cash in the short term

21   Which of the following statements best describes non-current assets?

   A   Assets which are used in the business over a number of accounting periods to undertake the activities of the organisation.

   B   Assets which are used to conduct the organisation's current business.

   C   Assets which are expected to be converted into cash in the short term.

   D   Assets which can be used to convert into cash in the short-term or to be used in the business over a number of accounting periods.

22   Which of the following statements best describes non-current liabilities?

   A   Liabilities which have not yet been incurred, but which will be incurred with the next twelve months.

   B   Liabilities which will only be paid upon termination of a business.

   C   Liabilities which will fall due for payment within twelve months of the reporting date.

   D   Liabilities which will fall due for payment after more than twelve months from the reporting date.

23   Which of the following statements best describes a current liability?

A   It is a liability which has not yet been incurred, but which will be incurred with the next twelve months.

B   It is a liability which will only be paid upon termination of a business.

C   It is a liability which will fall due for payment within twelve months of the reporting date.

D   It is a liability which will fall due for payment after more than twelve months from the reporting date.

24   Which of the following is not a book of prime entry?

A   The sales day book

B   The non-current assets register

C   The cash book

D   The journal

25   Which TWO of the following items is not a book of prime entry?

	Selected answer
Sales ledger	✓
The petty cash book	
The non-current asset register	✓
The purchase returns day book	

26   Dave receives goods which have been returned by a customer. In which book of prime entry will this be recorded?

A   The sales day book

B   The purchase returns day book

C   The sales returns day book

D   The journal

27   Martha returns goods to a supplier that where faulty. In which book of prime entry will this be recorded?

A   The sales day book

B   The purchase returns day book

C   The sales returns day book

D   The journal

28 What is the purpose of the books of prime entry?

A To ensure that accounting transactions are entered once in the accounting records

B To ensure that all sales transactions are recorded

C To ensure that all non-current assets are recorded

D To ensure that all transactions are recorded and summarised for inclusion in the general (nominal) ledger

29 Which TWO of the following items is not one of the components of a set of financial statements produced by a sole trader?

	Selected answer
Statement of financial position	
Bank statement	✓
Statement of profit or loss	
Supplier statement	✓

30 Which of the following statements best defines a statement of profit or loss?

A It is a summary of petty cash transactions

B It is a statement of assets and liabilities at a specific date

C It is a summary of bank receipts and payments

D It is a summary of revenue and expenses for a specified period of time

31 Which of the following statements best defines a statement of financial position?

A It is a summary of petty cash transactions

B It is a statement of assets and liabilities at a specific date

C It is a summary of bank receipts and payments

D It is a summary of revenue and expenses for a period of time

32 Which of the following statements provides a definition of an asset?

A It is an obligation to transfer economic resources resulting from a past transaction or event

B It is a resource controlled as a result of a past transaction or event from which economic resources are expected to be received

C It is the excess of revenue over expenses for a period of time

D It is the net investment in the business by the proprietor

33   **Which of the following statements provides a definition of a liability?**

A   It is an obligation to transfer economic resources resulting from a past transaction or event

B   It is a resource controlled as a result of a past transaction or event from which economic resources are expected to be received

C   It is the excess of revenue over expenses for a period of time

D   It is a decrease or outflow of economic benefits resulting from a transaction

34   **Which of the following statements provides a definition of capital?**

A   It is the accumulated profit in the business due to the proprietor

B   It is the capital introduced into the business by the proprietor

C   It is the net investment in the business by the proprietor

D   It is the accumulated profits less accumulated losses made by the business

35   **Which of the following items correctly represents the accounting equation?**

A   Assets = liabilities

B   Assets = Liabilities – proprietor's capital

C   Assets = proprietor's capital

D   Assets = Proprietor's capital + liabilities

36   **Which of the following statements best explains the accounting equation?**

A   The accounting equation demonstrates the effect of a transaction upon the assets, liabilities and proprietor's capital of a business.

B   The accounting equation demonstrates the impact a transaction on the statement of profit or loss for the year.

C   The accounting equation demonstrates the effect of a transaction upon the assets and income of a business.

D   The accounting equation demonstrates the effect of a transaction upon the expenses and liabilities of a business.

37   **What is the purpose of the sales day book?**

A   It records all cash and credit sale transactions in a sequential order so that they may be summarised and the totals posted to the nominal ledger at appropriate intervals.

B   It records all credit sales transactions in a sequential order so that they may be summarised and the totals posted to the nominal ledger at appropriate intervals.

C   It records of all cash sale transactions in a sequential order so that they may be summarised and the totals posted into the nominal ledger.

D   It records all credit sales transactions and all returns outwards transactions in a sequential order so that they may be summarised and the totals posted to the nominal ledger at appropriate intervals.

38   What is the purpose of the journal day book?

A   It records transactions that have not been captured or recorded in any other book of prime entry.

B   It captures all credit transactions in a sequential order so that they may be summarised and the totals posted to the nominal ledger at appropriate intervals.

C   It captures all cash transactions in a sequential order so that they may be summarised and the totals posted into the nominal ledger.

D   It captures all credit transactions and all returns outwards inwards and outwards transactions in a sequential order so that they may be summarised and the totals posted to the nominal ledger at appropriate intervals.

39   Which one of the following statements best explains proprietor's capital?

A   It is the amount of profit made by the business in the year

B   It is the amount of accumulated profits in the business

C   It is the net investment by the proprietor in the business

D   It is a business liability

40   Which of the following is a valid statement in relation to the reasons to close off the ledger accounts and produce a trial balance?

A   It is part of the double-entry accounting system.

B   It is a control to ensure that all transactions have been posted correctly to the correct ledger accounts.

C   It is a control to ensure that that the ledger accounts do not contain any errors.

D   It is a control to ensure that an equal value of debits and credits has been posted into the ledger accounts, but that there may still be errors within the ledger accounts.

41   What is the purpose of producing a trial balance?

A   It confirms that there are no errors in the accounting records.

B   It is a preliminary step prior to preparing financial statements to ensure that there are no obvious errors or omissions within the ledger accounts, although they may still contain errors.

C   It confirms whether or not the business has made a profit or loss for the year.

D   It confirms the proprietor's capital account balance at the end of the year.

42   A trial balance is made up of a list of debit balances and credit balances.

Which of the following statements is correct?

A   Every debit balance represents an expense

B   Assets are represented by debit balances

C   Liabilities are represented by debit balances

D   Income is included in the list of debit balances

43   What is the purpose of the purchase returns day book?

A   It records all returns inwards transactions in a sequential order so that they may be summarised and the totals posted to the nominal ledger at appropriate intervals.

B   It records all credit purchases transactions in a sequential order so that they may be summarised and the totals posted to the nominal ledger at appropriate intervals.

C   It records of all credit sales transactions in a sequential order so that they may be summarised and the totals posted into the nominal ledger.

D   It records all returns outwards transactions in a sequential order so that they may be summarised and the totals posted to the nominal ledger at appropriate intervals.

THE PREPARATION OF JOURNALS AND LEDGER ACCOUNTS

44   Which of the following best describes the entries that are made using the sales day book totals at the end of each month?

A   Debit sales with total net sales, credit receivables ledger control with total gross sales and credit sales tax with total sales tax.

B   Debit sales with total gross sales, credit receivables ledger control with total net sales and credit sales tax with total sales tax.

C   Debit receivables ledger control with total net sales, debit sales tax with total sales tax and credit sales with total gross sales.

D   Debit receivables ledger control with total gross sales, credit sales with total net sales and credit sales tax with total sales tax.

45   What accounting entries are required to record goods returned inwards if the original transaction was made on credit?

A   Debit Sales revenue, and   Credit Trade payables

B   Debit Returns inwards, and   Credit Trade payables

C   Debit Returns inwards, and   Credit Trade receivables

D   Debit Trade receivables, and   Credit Returns inwards

46   Which of the following best describes the entries relating to the totals from the receipts side of the cash book?

A   Debit bank with total receipts, credit cash sales, receivables ledger control and other with totals received.

B   Debit bank with total receipts, debit cash sales, and credit receivables ledger control and other with totals received.

C   Credit bank with total receipts, debit cash sales, receivables ledger control and other with totals received, credit discounts received with total cash discount and debit receivables ledger control with total cash discount.

D   Credit bank with total receipts, debit cash sales, receivables ledger control and other with totals received, credit discounts received with total cash discount and credit receivables ledger control with total cash discount.

47   Joe has prepared the following journal entry:

Debit	Cash	$850
Credit	T Sugden	$850

Which of the following is the correct narrative for the journal entry?

A   Cash sale to T Sugden

B   Cash purchase from T Sugden

C   Cash payment to T Sugden

D   Cash receipt from T Sugden

48   **Andrea started a taxi business by transferring her car, valued at $5,000, into the business. What accounting entries are required to record the transfer of the car into the business?**

A	Debit	Capital	Credit	Motor vehicle
B	Debit	Motor vehicle	Credit	Drawings
C	Debit	Motor vehicle	Credit	Capital
D	Debit	Motor vehicle	Credit	Bank

49   **Which of the following is the correct journal entry to write off an irrecoverable receivable?**

A	Debit	Sales	Credit	irrecoverable debts
B	Debit	Irrecoverable debts	Credit	Bank
C	Debit	Receivables	Credit	Irrecoverable debts
D	Debit	Irrecoverable debts	Credit	Receivables

50   Barclay had accounts receivable of $42,750 and $44,325 at 1 January 20X8 and 31 December 20X8 respectively.

During 20X8, cash sales of $265,000 and credit sales of $362,750 were made, contras with the payables ledger control account amounted to $18,750 and discounts received totalled 22,685. Irrecoverable debts of $8,640 were written off during 20X8 and Barclay wishes to retain its allowance for receivables at 5% of total receivables.

What was the cash received by Barclay from credit customers during the year?

A $336,935

B $352,535

C $329,850

D $333,785

51   **Wilson has returned goods which he bought on credit. What journal entry should Wilson make in his general ledger?**

A	Debit	Purchase returns	Credit	Trade payables
B	Debit	Trade payables	Credit	Bank
C	Debit	Bank	Credit	Trade payables
D	Debit	Trade payables	Credit	Purchase returns

RECORDING TRANSACTIONS AND EVENTS

52 **Which of the following is the correct formula to calculate cost of sales?**

A   Purchases – Opening inventory – Closing inventory

B   Purchases + Opening inventory + Closing inventory

C   Purchases – Opening inventory + Closing inventory

D   Purchases + Opening inventory – Closing inventory

53   Andrew's trial balance at 31 October 20X7 includes the following balances:

	$
Machinery at cost	85,800
Accumulated depreciation on machinery	21,750
Trade receivables	42,650
Receivables allowance	1,570
Bank overdraft	6,470
Inventory at 1 November 20X6	21,650

His inventory at 31 October 20X7 is valued at $22,300.

What value should be reported for current assets in Andrew's statement of financial position at 31 October 20X7?

A $62,730

B $63,380

C $64,950

D $69,850

54   Jamie is preparing his trial balance at 31 October 20X7. At 1 November 20X6 he had an accrual of $297 for telephone expenses. During the year to 31 October 20X7 he paid invoices for telephone charges up to 31 October 20X7 of $4,570.

What debit balance should Jamie include in his trial balance at 31 October 20X7 for telephone expenses?

$ 4273

The following information relates to questions 55 and 56:

The total amount owed to Robert by his customers at 30 November 20X7 was $78,600. Robert has decided that a balance of $600 should be written off as it is irrecoverable and that, based upon a review of receivables, an allowance equivalent to 1½% of the remaining receivables balance is required. His receivables allowance at 1 December 20X6 was $1,200.

Note: in the exam, all questions will be independent, and not based on a common scenario.

55   Robert has made the entry in the irrecoverable debts expense account to write off the irrecoverable balance.

What other entry does he need to make?

A   A debit entry in the sales account

B   A credit entry in the sales account

C   A debit entry in the receivables account

D   A credit entry in the receivables account

56   **How should the movement in the receivables allowance be reflected in the statement of profit or loss?**

A   A credit of $21

B   A charge of $21

C   A credit of $30

D   A charge of $30

57   **A business has capital of $10,000. Which of the following asset and liability figures could appear in this business' statement of financial position?**

A	Assets	$6,000	Liabilities	$16,000
B	Assets	$6,000	Liabilities	$4,000
C	Assets	$10,000	Liabilities	$10,000
D	Assets	$14,000	Liabilities	$4,000

58   A business commenced with capital in cash of $1,000. Inventory costing $800 (zero sales tax) is purchased on credit, and half of that was sold for $1,000 plus sales tax at 20%, the customer paying in cash immediately.

What will be the accounting equation after these transactions?

A   Assets $1,800 less Liabilities $200 equals Capital $1,600

B   Assets $2,200 less Liabilities $1,000 equals Capital $1,200

C   Assets $2,600 less Liabilities $800 equals Capital $1,800

D   Assets $2,600 less Liabilities $1,000 equals Capital $1,600

59 A sole trader had opening capital of $10,000 and closing capital of $4,500. During the period, the owner introduced capital of $4,000 and withdrew $8,000 for her own use.

What was the loss for the year?

$ 1,500

60 At 31 May 20X7 Roberta's trial balance included the following items:

	$
Inventory at 1 June 20X6	23,856
Trade receivables	55,742
Trade payables	32,165
Bank overdraft	5,855
Loan due for repayment in 20X9	15,000

What was the value of Roberta's current liabilities at 31 May 20X7?

$ 38,020

61 A business returned goods that had a net value of $800 to Rawlins. What would be the debit to Rawlins' account if sales tax is payable at a rate of 10% by the business?

A $720.00

B $800.00

C $880.00

D $969.70

62 A summary of the transactions of Ramsgate, who is registered for sales tax at 15%, showed the following for the month of August 20X9.

Outputs $60,000 (exclusive of sales tax)

Inputs $46,000 (inclusive of sales tax)

At the beginning of the period Ramsgate owed $3,400 to the government tax authorities, and during the period he has paid $2,600 to them.

What was the amount owed to the government tax authorities at the end of the accounting period?

$ 3,800

The following information relates to questions 63 to 65.

The following information was extracted from the books of Miss Fitt at 31 December 20X8:

	$
Sales	18,955
Cost of sales	11,334
Salaries and wages	2,447
Motor expenses	664
Rent	456
Rates	120
Insurance	146
Packing expenses	276
Lighting and heating expenses	665
Sundry expenses	115
Motor vehicles	2,400
Fixtures and fittings	600
Inventory as at 31 December 20X8	4,998
Receivables	4,577
Payables	3,045
Cash in bank	3,876
Cash in hand	120
Capital	10,794

Note: in the exam, all questions will be independent, and not based on a common scenario.

63   **What is the current liabilities figure in the statement of financial position at 31 December 20X8?**

$ 3045

64   **What is the non-current assets figure at 31 December 20X8?**

$ 3000

65   **What is the net profit for the year ended 31 December 20X8?**

$ 2732

66   **How is closing inventory recorded in the bookkeeping records?**

A   By a debit to inventory and a credit to profit or loss

B   By a debit to profit or loss and a credit to inventory

C   By a debit to inventory and a credit to purchases

D   By writing the figure in a note beneath the trial balance

67   **How is the closing balance on accounts receivable included in the statement of financial position?**

A   By a debit to accounts receivable and a credit to statement of financial position

B   By a debit to statement of financial position and a credit to accounts receivable

C   By a debit to statement of financial position

D   By writing the total in the statement of financial position, the balance on accounts receivable remaining unaffected

68   Anthony received goods which cost $250 from Brad on credit terms and Anthony subsequently paid by cheque. Anthony then discovered that the goods were faulty and cancelled the cheque before it was recorded and cashed by Brad.

What accounting entries should Anthony use to record the cancellation of the cheque in his books?

A   Debit Accounts payable, and   Credit Returns outwards

B   Debit Bank, and   Credit Accounts payable

C   Debit Bank, and   Credit Accounts payable

D   Debit Accounts payable, and   Credit Returns outwards

69   **Which of the following is a bank overdraft an example of?**

A   An asset

B   A liability

C   Revenue

D   Expense

70   Simon, who is a sole trader, made a profit of $22,860 in the year to 30 November 20X5. During the year his drawings were $16,890. At 1 December 20X4 the balance on his capital account was $68,920.

What is the balance on Simon's capital account at 30 November 20X5?

$ 74 890

71   At 30 November 20X5 Jenny had a bank loan of $8,500 and a balance of $678 in hand in her bank account.

How should these amounts be recorded on Jenny's opening trial balance at 1 December 20X5?

A   Debit $7,822

B   Credit $7,822

C   Credit $8,500 and Debit $678

D   Debit $8,500 and Credit $678

72 During May 20X7, Sarah's purchases were $126,500, and her sales were $150,000. Sarah's gross profit margin is 20% of sales. The value of her inventory at 1 May 20X7 was $12,500.

What was the value of Sarah's inventory at 31 May 20X7?

$ _19000_

73 At 31 May 20X6 Dave's capital balance was $96,578. During the year to 31 May 20X7, his drawings were 25,764. At 31 May 20X7 his capital balance was $104,864.

What was Dave's profit for the year ended 31 May 20X7?

$ _34 000_

74 A business borrowed $1,700 from its bank, and used the cash to buy a new computer.

How is the accounting equation affected following these transactions?

	Assets	Liabilities
A	Unchanged	Decreased
B	Unchanged	Increased
C	Increased	Increased
D	Increased	Decreased

75 In the year to 31 May 20X6, Julie paid $2,500 for property repairs. Her bookkeeper treated this as capital expenditure.

What is the effect of this error on Julie's profit for the year to 31 may 20X6, and the value of assets at that date?

	Profit	Assets
A	Understated	Overstated
B	Understated	Understated
C	Overstated	Overstated
D	Overstated	Understated

76 Edith estimated that, at 31 May 20X6, she had the following assets and liabilities:

	$
Non-current assets	33,750
Inventory	4,845
Trade receivables	11,248
Trade payables	9,633
Bank overdraft	539

Upon checking, you note that she also has a prepayment for rent of $520.

What is Edith's capital account balance at 31 May 20X6?

$ _40191_

77 At 31 October 20X6 Janine had an outstanding balance of $24,000 on her bank loan account. The terms of the loan require her to repay $400 on the first day of each month.

How should the loan be reported on Janine's statement of financial position at 31 October 20X6?

	Current liability	Non-current liability
A	nil	$24,000
B	$24,000	nil
C	$19,200	$4,800
D	$4,800	$19,200

78 Owen allows customers to return faulty goods within 14 days of purchase. At 30 November 20X5 he made a provision of $6,548 for sales returns. At 30 November 20X6 he calculated that his provision should be $7,634.

What should be reported in Owen's statement of profit or loss for the year to 30 November 20X6 in relation to this provision?

A A charge of $7,634

B A credit of $7,634

C A charge of $1,086

D A credit of $1,086

79 At 31 October 20X6 Roger's trial balance included the following balances:

	$
Machinery at cost	12,890
Accumulated depreciation	8,950
Inventory	5,754
Trade receivables	11,745
Trade payables	7,830
Bank overdraft	1,675
Cash at bank	150

What was the carrying amount of Roger's current assets at 31 October 20X6?

$ 17 649

80 At 1 May 20X7 Brian had an opening accrual of $353 for motor expenses. During the year to 30 April 20X8 he paid invoices for motor expenses with a total value of $4,728. He has no closing accrual or prepayment at 30 April 20X8.

What balance should Brian enter on his trial balance for motor expenses?

A $4,375 debit

B $4,375 credit

C $5,081 debit

D $5,081 credit

81   The balance on Jane's payables' ledger control account is $31,554. Jane has discovered that she has not recorded:

- a settlement discount of $53 received from a supplier; and
- a supplier's invoice for $622.

What amount should be reported for payables in Jane's statement of financial position?

A $30,879

B $30,985

C $32,123

D $32,229

82   At his year end, Keith had accrued expenses totalling $4,176 and prepaid expenses totalling $3,718.

How should the accrued and prepaid expenses be reported on Keith's statement of financial position?

A   As a current asset of $458

B   As a current liability of $458

C   As a current asset of $4,176 and a current liability of $3,718

D   As a current asset of $3,718 and a current liability of $4,176

83   **Which of the following is the correct journal entry to record a credit note issued to a customer who returned goods, having purchased them on credit?**

A   Debit Sales returns, and   Credit   Cash

B   Debit Cash, and   Credit   Sales returns

C   Debit Trade receivables, and Credit   Sales returns

D   Debit Sales returns, and   Credit   Trade receivables

84   Peter's trial balance at 30 September 20X4 included the following balances:

	$
Machinery at cost	96,400
Accumulated depreciation on machinery	23,500
Trade receivables	48,325
Receivables allowance	1,840
Bank overdraft	7,360
Inventory at 1 October 20X3	23,200

His inventory at 30 September 20X4 was valued at $25,700.

What carrying amount should be reported for current assets at 30 September 20X4?

$ 72,185

85 Pavel's trial balance at 30 June 20X6 included the following balances:

	$
Trade payables	38,975
Accumulated depreciation on machinery	24,200
Trade receivables	48,325
Allowance for receivables	3,200
Bank overdraft	6,125
Bank loan due for repayment 30 June 20X9	40,000

What carrying amount should be reported for current liabilities in Pavel's statement of financial position at 30 June 20X6?

$ 45,00

86 Jane is preparing her trial balance at 31 March 20X3. At 1 April 20X2 she had an accrual of $327 for heat and light charges. During the year to 31 March 20X3 she paid invoices for heat and light charges up to 31 March 20X3 of $8,750.

What balance should Jane include in her trial balance at 31 March 20X3 for heat and light charges?

A $9,077 debit

B $8,423 credit

C $8,423 debit

D $9,077 credit

The following information relates to questions 87 and 88:

The total amount owed to Mary by her customers at 31 December 20X5 was $83,200. Mary has decided that a balance of $1,825 should be written off as it is irrecoverable, and that, following a review of accounts receivables balances, an allowance of $6,510 is required at 31 December 20X5. Her receivables allowance at 1 January 20X5 was $8,200.

Note: in the exam, all questions will be independent, and not based on a common scenario.

---

87 **Mary has made the entry in the expense account to write off the irrecoverable balance. What other accounting entry does Mary need to make?**

A   A debit entry in the sales account

B   A credit entry in the sales account

C   A debit entry in the receivables account

D   A credit entry in the receivables account

88 **How should the movement in the receivables allowance be reflected in the statement of profit or loss?**

A   A credit of $1,544

B   A charge of $1,544

C   A credit of $1,690

D   A charge of $1,690

89 A business had total assets of $25,000. Which of the following capital and liability figures could appear in this business' statement of financial position?

A	Capital	$10,000	Liabilities	$35,000
B	Capital	$10,000	Liabilities	$15,000
C	Capital	$18,000	Liabilities	$43,000
D	Capital	$40,000	Liabilities	$15,000

90 A sole trader had opening capital of $18,000 and closing capital of $6,900. During the accounting period, the owner introduced capital of $6,000 and withdrew $10,000 for her own use.

What was her loss for the accounting period?

$ - 7,100

91 West returned goods to Sprake that had a net value of $560. What was the value of the debit entry to Sprake's account in West's accounting records if sales tax is payable at a rate of 20%?

$ 672

92 A summary of the transactions of Kent, who is registered for sales tax at 20%, shows the following for the month of July 20X1:

Outputs $90,000 (exclusive of sales tax) and   Inputs $75,000 (inclusive of sales tax)

At the beginning of the month Kent owed $4,275 to the government tax authority, and during the month he paid $4,100 to the tax authority.

What was the amount owing to the government tax authority at the end of the month?

$ 5,675

The following information relates to questions 93 to 96:

The following information was extracted from the books of Miss Trust at 30 June 20X4:

	$
Sales	21,370
Cost of sales	12,413
Salaries and wages	3,560
Motor expenses	572
Rent	600
Rates	150
Lighting and heating expenses	702
Sundry expenses	113
Motor vehicles	7,200
Fixtures and fittings	1,000
Inventory as at 30 June 20X4	5,243
Receivables	6,715
Payables	3,115
Cash in hand	115
Overdraft	350
Capital	13,548

Note: in the exam, all questions will be independent, and not based on a common scenario.

93   What carrying amount for current liabilities should be included in the statement of financial position at 30 June 20X4?

     A $3,115

     B $3,465

     C $3,345

     D $2,765

94   What carrying amount for non-current assets should be included in the statement of financial position as at 30 June 20X4?

     $ 8 2 0 0

95   What was the net profit for the year ended 30 June 20X4?

     $ 3 2 6 0

96   What carrying amount for current assets should be included in the statement of financial position as at 30 June 20X4?

     A $11,858

     B $11,958

     C $11,723

     D $12,073

97 **What are the accounting entries required to record goods returned outwards?**

A   Debit sales account and credit returns outwards account

B   Debit returns outwards account and credit receivables account

C   Debit returns outwards account and credit payables account

D   Debit payables account and credit returns outwards account

98 Oxford had a total accounts receivable balance of $84,700 at 1 May 20X6 and $82,500 at 30 June 20X7. During the year ended 30 June 20X7, there were cash sales of $86,400 and cash received from receivables of $564,250. During the year ended 30 June 20X7, contras with the payables ledger control account amounted to $8,300 and discounts received totalled $17,260. Irrecoverable receivables of $12,650 were written off and Oxford wishes to have an allowance for receivables of $3,300 at 30 June 20X7.

What value of credit sales were made in the year ended 30 June 20X2?

$  583 000

99 A trial balance is made up of a list of debit balances and credit balances.

Which of the following statements is correct?

A   Every debit balance represents an asset

B   Assets are represented by credit balances

C   Liabilities are represented by credit balances

D   Income is included in the list of debit balances

100 During June 20X9, Mike's purchases were $160,000, and his sales were $180,000. Mike's gross profit is 10% of sales. The value of his inventory at 1 June 20X9 was $20,000.

What was the value of Mike's inventory at 30 June 20X9?

$  180 00 .

101 At 1 May 20X5 Martha's capital balance was $89,627. During the year to 30 April 20X6, her profit for the year was $32,678. At 30 April 20X6 her capital balance was $98,473.

What were Martha's drawings for the year ended 30 April 20X6?

$ 23832

102 In the year ended 31 January 20X5, Hannah paid $3,700 for new fixtures and fittings. Her bookkeeper treated this as revenue expenditure.

What is the effect of this error on Hannah's profit for the year to 31 may 20X6, and the value of assets at that date?

	Profit	Assets
A	Understated	Overstated
B	Understated	Understated
C	Overstated	Overstated
D	Overstated	Understated

103 Ellie estimated that, at 31 August 20X4, she had the following assets and liabilities:

	$
Non-current assets	33,750
Inventory	4,845
Trade receivables	11,248
Trade payables	9,633
Bank overdraft	539

Upon checking this information, you note that she also had an accrual for rent of £750 which had not been accounted for.

What was the balance on Ellie's capital account at 31 August 20X4?

$ 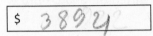 38924

104 A business commenced with capital of $3,500 in cash. Inventory was purchased on credit at a cost of $2,500 (zero sales tax), and half of that was sold for $3,000 plus sales tax at 10%, the customer paying in cash immediately.

What was the accounting equation resulting from these transactions?

A Assets $5,250 less Liabilities $300 equals Capital $4,950

B Assets $4,000 less Liabilities $300 equals Capital $3,700

C Assets $8,050 less Liabilities $2,800 equals Capital $5,250

D Assets $4,550 less Liabilities $300 equals Capital $4,250

105 At 31 December 20X5, a sole trader had a closing capital balance of $15,250. During the year ended 31 December 20X5, the sole trader introduced capital of $3,800 and withdrew $7,300 for his own use. The business made a profit for the year ended 31 December 20X5 of $8,500.

What was the opening capital balance at 1 January 20X5?

$ 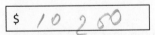 10 250

106 At 31 May 20X7 Victoria's trial balance included the following items:

	$
Inventory at 1 June 20X6	23,056
Trade receivables	55,742
Trade payables	32,165
Petty cash balance	100
Bank overdraft	5,855
Fixtures and fittings	15,000

Based upon the available information, what was the value of Victoria's current assets at 31 May 20X7?

$ 50842

107 ABC Co sold goods with a list price of $1,000 to Smith which was subject to trade discount of 5% and early settlement discount of 4% if the invoice was paid within 7 days. The normal credit period available to credit customers is 30 days from invoice date. Based upon past experience, Smith has never taken advantage of early settlement terms and has always paid after 30 days.

If Smith subsequently pays within 7 days and is eligible for the settlement discount, what accounting entries should be made by ABC Co to record settlement of the amount outstanding?

A   Debit Cash $950, Debit Revenue $50 and Credit Trade receivables $1,000

B   Debit Cash $950, Credit Revenue$38 and Credit Trade receivables $912

C   Debit Cash $912, Debit Revenue $38 and Credit Trade receivables $950

D   Debit Cash $912, and Credit Trade receivables $912

108 ABC Co sold goods with a list price of $2,500 to Jones which was subject to trade discount of 5% and early settlement discount of 4% if the invoice was paid within 7 days. The normal credit period available to credit customers is 30 days from invoice date. Based upon past experience, Jones always takes advantage of early settlement terms.

If Jones subsequently pays within 7 days and is eligible for the settlement discount, what accounting entries should be made by ABC Co to record settlement of the amount outstanding?

A   Debit Cash $2,280, Debit Revenue $95 and Credit Trade receivables $2,375

B   Debit Cash $2,280 and Credit Trade receivables $2,280

C   Debit Cash $2,375, Debit Revenue $125 and Credit Trade receivables $2,500

D   Debit Cash $2,500, and Credit Trade receivables $2,500

109 ABC Co sold goods with a list price of $4,500 to Black which was subject to trade discount of 5% and early settlement discount of 4% if the invoice was paid within 7 days. The normal credit period available to credit customers is 30 days from invoice date. Based upon past experience, Black always takes advantage of early settlement terms.

If, on this occasion, Black subsequently pays after 7 days and is not eligible for the settlement discount, what accounting entries should be made by ABC Co to record settlement of the amount outstanding?

A   Debit Cash $4,104, Debit Revenue $396 and Credit Trade receivables $4,500

B   Debit Cash $4,275, Debit Revenue $171 and Credit Trade receivables $4,104

C   Debit Cash $4,275 and Credit Trade receivables $4,275

D   Debit Cash $4,275, Credit Trade receivables $4,104 and Credit Revenue $171

110 ABC Co sold goods with a list price of $3,700 to White which was subject to trade discount of 5% and early settlement discount of 4% if the invoice was paid within 7 days. The normal credit period available to credit customers is 30 days from invoice date. Based upon past experience, White does not normally pay early to take advantage of early settlement terms.

If, as expected, White subsequently pays after 30 days, what accounting entries should be made by ABC Co to record settlement of the amount outstanding?

A Debit Cash $3,515, and Credit Trade receivables $3,515

B Debit Cash $3,515, Credit Discount received $140.60 and Credit Trade receivables $3,374.40

C Debit Cash $3,374.40 and Credit Trade receivables $3,374.40

D Debit Cash $3,515, Debit Revenue $185 and Credit Trade receivables $3,700

111 ABC Co sold goods with a list price of $1,400 to Green which was subject to trade discount of 4% and early settlement discount of 5% if the invoice was paid within 7 days. The normal credit period available to credit customers is 30 days from invoice date. Based upon past experience, Green has always taken advantage of early settlement terms and has always paid within 7 days.

If, on this occasion, Green subsequently pays after 30 days, what accounting entries should be made by ABC Co to record settlement of the amount outstanding?

A Debit Cash $1,344.00, Credit Trade receivables $1,276.80 and Credit Revenue $67.20

B Debit Cash $1,400 Credit Trade receivables $1,400

C Debit Cash $1,344 and Credit Trade receivables $1,344

D Debit Cash $1,276.80, and Credit Trade receivables $1,276.80

INVENTORIES

112 Tim has recently commenced trading. The materials he uses in his business are subject to regular price rises. He is unsure how to value his inventory and is trying to decide whether to use 'first In, first out' (FIFO), or continuous weighted average.

Which of the following statements is correct?

A Tim's profit will be unaffected by the method of inventory valuation

B FIFO will lead to the higher reported profit

C Continuous weighted average will lead to the higher reported profit

D The profit will be more accurate if FIFO is used

113 You are preparing the final accounts for a business. The cost of the items in closing inventory is $41,875. This includes some items which cost $1,960 and which were damaged in transit. You have estimated that it will cost $360 to repair the items, and that the items could then be sold for $1,200.

What was the correct inventory valuation for inclusion in the final accounts?

$ 40 755

114   Bill uses the first in, first out method of inventory valuation. At 1 May 20X8 he had 60 units in inventory at a total value of $1,320. The movement on his inventory in May 20X8 was:

Receipts	14 May	120 units at $22.20
	26 May	150 units at $22.30
Sales	18 May	90 units
	28 May	80 units

What was the value of Bill's inventory at 31 May 20X8?

$ 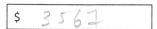 3567

115   Mark uses the periodic weighted average method of inventory valuation. At 1 August 20X6 he had 60 units in inventory at a total value of $1,320. The inventory movements during August 20X6 were as follows:

Receipts	14 Aug	120 units at $22.50 per unit
	26 Aug	150 units at $23.36 per unit
Sales	18 Aug	90 units
	28 Aug	80 units

What was the value of Mark's inventory at 31 August 20X6?

$  3648

116   Daniel uses the continuous weighted average cost method of inventory valuation. At 1 February 20X4 he had 60 units in inventory at a total value of $1,320. The inventory movements during February 20X4 were as follows:

Receipts	14 Feb	180 units at $23.00 per unit
Sales	18 Feb	90 units at $30.00 per unit

What was the value of Daniel's inventory at 28 February 20X4?

A $3,300.00

B $3,390.00

C $3,412.50

D $3,450.00

117   Davina uses the continuous weighted average cost method of inventory valuation. At 1 April 20X5 she had 120 units in inventory at a unit cost of $22.00. The inventory movements during April 20X5 were as follows:

Receipts	15 Apr	360 units at $23.00 per unit
Sales	25 Apr	300 units at $32.00 per unit

What was Davina's cost of sales for the month of April 20X5?

$ 6825

118 An item of inventory was purchased for $500. It is expected to be sold for $1,200 although $250 will need to be spent on it in order to achieve the sale. To replace the same item of inventory would cost $650.

At what value should this item of inventory be valued in the financial statements?

$  500

119 Ajay's financial year end is 30 June 20X6. However, the annual inventory count took place on 7 July 20X6. The inventory value on that date was $38,950. During the period from 30 June 20X6 to 7 July 20X6, the following transactions took place:

Sales $6,500

Purchases $4,250

Sales are made at a mark-up on cost of 25%.

What was Ajay's inventory valuation at 30 June 20X6?

A $36,700

B $41,200

C $39,900

D $38,000

120 Percy Pilbeam is a book wholesaler. On each sale, commission of 4% is payable to the selling agent. The following information is available in respect of total inventories of three of his most popular titles at his financial year-end:

	Cost	Selling price
	$	$
Henry VII – Shakespeare	2,280	2,900
Dissuasion – Jane Armstrong-Siddeley	4,080	4,000
Pilgrim's Painful Progress – John Bunion	1,280	1,300

What was the total value of these items of inventory in Percy's statement of financial position?

A $7,368

B $7,400

C $7,560

D $7,640

121 An organisation's inventory at 1 July is 15 units at a cost of $3.00 each. The following subsequent movements occur:

3 July 20X4   5 units sold at $3.30 each

8 July 20X4   10 units bought at $3.50 each

12 July 20X4   8 units sold at $4.00 each

At what valuation will closing inventory be included in the financial statements at 31 July, using the first in, first out, method of inventory valuation?

A $31.50

B $36.00

C $39.00

D $41.00

122 Nigel has closing inventory which cost $38,750. This includes some damaged items which cost $3,660. It will cost Nigel $450 to repair these. He will be able to sell them for $1,500 after the repairs are completed.

What is the correct value of Nigel's closing inventory?

A $35,090

B $36,140

C $36,590

D $38,750

123 **Which method of inventory valuation is used when issues are assumed to be taken from inventory in the order in which they were received?**

A   Net realisable value

B   First in, first out

C   Periodic weighted average

D   Continuous weighted average

124 When she prepared her draft accounts, Wilma included her closing inventory at a value of $21,870. She has just found out that some items valued at $2,150 had not been included in the calculation.

How will net profit and net assets be affected when the inventory valuation is corrected?

	Net profit	Net assets
A	Reduced by $2,150	Reduced by £2,150
B	Reduced by $2,140	Increased by $2,150
C	Increased by $2,150	Reduced by $2,150
D	Increased by $2,150	Increased by $2,150

125 Colin made a mistake in his calculations which resulted in the value of his closing inventory at 30 April 20X4 being overstated by $900. The value was calculated correctly at 30 April 20X5.

What was the effect of the error on the profit reported in Colin's accounts for each of the two years?

	20X4	*20X5*
A	Overstated by $900	Not affected
B	Overstated by $900	Understated by $900
C	Understated by $900	Not affected
D	Understated by $900	Overstated by $900

126 Kieron is an antiques dealer. His inventory includes a clock which cost $15,800. Kieron expects to spend $700 on repairing the clock which will mean that he will be able to sell it for $26,000.

At what value should the clock be included in Kieron's inventory?

$ 15800

127 LMN has just published its financial statements, which show a gross profit for the year of $6.5 million. A major error in the inventory valuation has just been discovered. The opening inventory was overstated by $1.3 million, and the closing inventory has been understated by $1.6 million.

What should be LMN's correct gross profit for the year?

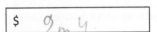

$ 9m 4

128 **What is the unit cost of the following item?**

	$
Raw materials	5.00
Labour	3.00
Manufacturing overheads	1.00
Variable administrative overheads	2.50

A	$5.00
B	$8.00
C	$9.00
D	$11.50

129 Daniel made an error when he calculated the value of his closing inventory, which resulted in an overvaluation of inventory.

How will his net profit for the year and net assets at the end of the year be affected by this error?

	Net profit	Net assets
A	Overstated	Understated
B	Overstated	Overstated
C	Understated	Understated
D	Understated	Overstated

130 **What is the net realisable value of the following item?**

	$
Selling price	20.00
Packaging costs	2.00
Delivery costs	3.00
Licence fee paid after delivery	2.50

$ _____ 12.00

131 Diesel fuel included in the inventory at 1 November 20X7 was $12,500 and there were invoices awaited for $1,700. During the year to 31 October 20X8, diesel fuel bills of $85,400 were paid, and a delivery worth $1,300 had yet to be invoiced. At 31 October 20X8, the inventory of diesel fuel was valued at $9,800.

What amount is to be charged to the statement of profit or loss for the year to 31 October 20X8 for diesel fuel?

$ _____

132 Suresh & Co sells three products – Basic, Super and Luxury. The following information was available at the year-end:

	Basic	Super	Luxury
	$ per unit	$ per unit	$ per unit
Original cost	6	9	18
Estimated selling price	9	12	15
Selling and distribution costs	1	4	5
	Units	Units	Units
Units held	200	250	150

What should be the valuation of inventory at the end of the year?

$ _____ 4700

133 In times of rising prices, what will be the effect upon profit and closing inventory valuation using the first in, first out method of inventory valuation in comparison to the average cost method of inventory valuation?

    A   A higher profit and a lower closing inventory value

    B   A higher profit and a higher closing inventory value

    C   A lower profit and a lower closing inventory value

    D   A lower profit and a higher inventory value

134 Arlene valued her inventory at 30 June 20X1 at its cost of $22,960. This included some items which cost $1,950 which have been difficult to sell. Arlene intends to have these items repacked at a cost of $400. She then expects to sell them for $900.

What was the value of closing inventory in Arlene's accounts at 30 June 20X1?

$

135 At 30 November 20X1 Kim's inventory was valued at its cost of $22,700. This includes items costing $1,300 which have been superseded by an updated design. Kim will be able to sell these items through an agent for $700. The agent's commission will be 10% of selling price.

What was the value of closing inventory on 30 November 20X1?

$

136 Mylee uses the periodic weighted average method of inventory valuation. At 1 November 20X7 she had 60 units in inventory at a total value of $1,320. The inventory movements during August 20X6 were as follows:

Receipts	14 Nov	150 units at $20.00 per unit
	26 Nov	100 units at $25.00 per unit
Sales	18 Nov	80 units sold for $30 per unit
	28 Nov	90 units sold for $30 per unit

What was the value of Mylee's inventory at 30 November 20X7?

    A $6,820

    B $3,740

    C $3,080

    D $1,760

137 Danielle uses the continuous weighted average cost method of inventory valuation. At 1 April 20X9 she had 50 units in inventory at a total value of $815. The inventory movements during February 20X4 were as follows:

Receipts	14 Apr	270 units at $19.50 per unit
Sales	18 Apr	180 units at $35.00 per unit

What was the cost of goods sold by Danielle for the month of April 20X9?

$

NON-CURRENT ASSETS AND DEPRECIATION

138 What is the accounting concept that specifies non-current assets should be valued at cost less accumulated depreciation, rather than at their enforced saleable value?

A   Net realisable value concept

B   Prudence concept

C   Realisation concept

D   Going concern concept

139 **What is the purpose of charging depreciation in the accounts of a business?**

A   To ensure that funds are available for the eventual replacement of the asset.

B   To reduce the cost of the asset in the statement of financial position to its estimated market value.

C   To allocate the cost of the non-current asset over the accounting periods expected to benefit from its use.

D   To comply with the prudence concept.

140 An asset cost $100,000. It is expected to last for ten years and have a scrap value of $10,000. The business is going to depreciate this asset at 20% on the reducing balance basis.

What will the depreciation charge on this asset be in its second year?

A $14,400

B $16,000

C $18,000

D $20,000

141 **Which TWO of the following are reasons for maintaining a non-current asset register?**

	Selected answer
To calculate the total balance outstanding on loans raised to purchase non-current assets	
To help in carrying out the physical verification of non-current assets	✓
To calculate the profit or loss on disposal of non-current assets	✓
To eliminate the need to maintain ledger accounts relating to non-current assets	

142 Esther is recording the invoice for the purchase of a new plant and equipment.

Which TWO of the following items should be capitalised as part of the cost of the asset?

	Selected answer
Cost of staff training to use the new plant and equipment	
Installation costs	✓
Three-year maintenance agreement	
Delivery costs	✓

143 The opening balance on Derv's motor vehicles at cost account was $140,000. The opening balance on depreciation of motor vehicles was $60,000. The business purchased new vehicles costing $30,000 during the year. No vehicles were sold. The business depreciates vehicles at 25% on the reducing balance basis, with a full year's depreciation in the year of acquisition and none in the year of disposal.

What is the closing balance on Derv 's depreciation of motor vehicles account?

$ [   ]

144 **Which of the following provides a definition of a non-current asset register?**

A   It is an alternative name for the non-current asset ledger account.

B   It is a list of the physical non-current assets rather than their financial cost.

C   It is a schedule of planned maintenance of non-current assets for use by the plant engineer.

D   It is a schedule of the cost and other information about each individual non-current asset.

145 An organisation's non-current asset register shows a net book value of $125,600. The non-current asset account in the general ledger shows a net book value of $135,600.

What would explain the difference if it is due to a disposed asset not having been deducted from the non-current assets ledger?

A   There were disposal proceeds of $15,000 and a profit on disposal of $5,000

B   There were disposal proceeds of $15,000 and a carrying amount of $5,000

C   There were disposal proceeds of $15,000 and a loss on disposal of $5,000

D   There were disposal proceeds of $5,000 and a carrying amount of $5,000

The following information relates to questions 146 and 147.

Arnold bought a machine for use in his business on 1 November 20X4. He gave the supplier a cheque for $11,570 and traded in an old machine. The supplier allowed him $4,430 in part exchange for the old machine. Arnold depreciates machinery on the reducing balance basis at a rate of 20% per annum. The old machine had cost $12,000 and had been depreciated by $5,856.

Note: in the exam, all questions will be independent, and not based on a common scenario.

146   **What was the profit or loss on the trade in of the old machine?**

A   A profit of $1,426

B   A profit of $1,714

C   A loss of $1,426

D   A loss of $1,714

147   **What was the depreciation charge on the new machine for the year to 31 October 20X5?**

$ 3200

148   Information relating to two non-current assets was as follows:

	Cost	Accumulated depreciation at 1 January 20X4	Depreciation charge for 20X4
	$	$	$
Asset 1	100,000	50,000	7,500
Asset 2	50,000	10,000	7,500

Which depreciation method has been applied to each asset?

	15% straight-line	15% reducing balance
Asset 1		✓
Asset 2	✓	

149   When Michelle purchased a new car, she used her old car in part exchange. She has made the correct entry for the part-exchange value of $3,500 in the non-current asset disposal account.

What other entry is needed to complete the double entry for the part-exchange value of $3,500?

A   A debit entry in the motor vehicles at cost account

B   A credit entry in the motor vehicles at cost account

C   A debit entry in the bank account

D   A credit entry in the bank account

150 On 1 July 20X4 Tom bought a machine for $15,500. He depreciates machinery at a rate of 20% per annum on the reducing balance basis. A full year's depreciation is charged in the year an asset is purchased. His year end is 31 October.

What was the depreciation charge on the machine for the year to 31 October 20X6?

$ _1984_

151 **Which of the following would normally be recorded in a non-current asset register?**

(i)   the location of each asset

(ii)   the serial number of each asset

(iii)   accumulated depreciation on each asset.

A   (i) only

B   (ii) and (iii) only

C   (i) and (iii) only

D   (i), (ii) and (iii)

152 Ed's year end is 30 September. He depreciates office furniture at 15% per annum on the straight line basis. A full year's depreciation is charged in the year an asset is purchased, and no depreciation is charged in the year it is sold. In March 20X5 Ed bought office furniture for $80,000.

If he sells the office furniture for $39,000 in July 20X8, what will be Ed's profit or loss on disposal?

A   A profit of $7,000

B   A loss of $7,000

C   A profit of $5,000

D   A loss of $5,000

153 On 1 January 20X7, a business purchased an item of plant. The invoice showed:

	$
Cost of plant	48,000
Delivery to factory	400
One year warranty covering breakdown	800
	———
	49,200
	———

In addition, modifications to the factory building costing $2,200 were necessary to enable the plant to be installed.

What amount should be capitalised for the plant in the accounting records of the business?

$ _50 600_

154 A non-current asset was purchased at the beginning of Year 1 for $2,400 and depreciated by 20% per annum using the reducing balance method. At the beginning of Year 4 it was sold for $1,200.

What was the profit or loss on disposal?

A   A loss on disposal of $240.00

B   A loss on disposal of $28.80

C   A profit on disposal of $28.80

D   A profit on disposal of $240.00

155 A business' non-current assets had a carrying value of $125,000. An asset which had cost $12,000 was sold for $9,000, at a profit of $2,000.

What was the revised carrying amount of non-current assets?

$

156 A non-current asset was disposed of for $2,200 during the last accounting year. It had been purchased exactly three years earlier for $5,000, with an expected residual value of $500, and had been depreciated on the reducing balance basis, at 20% per annum.

What was the loss on disposal?

$

157 **Which TWO of the following items should not be accounted for as capital expenditure?**

	Selected answer
The purchase of a car for a member of the sales department to visit clients	
The purchase of a car for resale by a car dealer	✓
Legal fees incurred on the purchase of a building	
The cost of painting a building	✓

158 A car was purchased for $12,000 on 1 April 20X1 and has been depreciated at 20% each year straight line, assuming no residual value. The accounting policy of the business is to charge a full year's depreciation in the year of purchase and no depreciation in the year of sale. The car was traded in for a replacement vehicle on 1 August 20X4 for an agreed figure of $5,000.

What was the profit on the disposal of the vehicle for the year ended 31 December 20X4?

$

159 A business accounted for the repair of an item of plant and machinery as capital expenditure in the accounting records.

What is the effect of this error upon the profit for the year and also upon the carrying value of assets included in the statement of financial position before the error is corrected?

A   Profit for the year is understated and assets on the statement of financial position are overstated.

B   Profit for the year is overstated and assets on the statement of financial position are overstated.

C   Profit for the year is understated and assets on the statement of financial position are understated.

D   Profit for the year is overstated and assets on the statement of financial position are understated.

160 A business accounted for the purchase of a new delivery truck as a motor expense in the accounting records.

What is the effect of this error upon the profit for the year and also upon the carrying value of assets included in the statement of financial position before the error is corrected?

A   Profit for the year is understated and assets on the statement of financial position are overstated.

B   Profit for the year is overstated and assets on the statement of financial position are overstated.

C   Profit for the year is understated and assets on the statement of financial position are understated.

D   Profit for the year is overstated and assets on the statement of financial position are understated.

161 Smart purchased an item of plant at a cost of $100,000 in 1 January 20X2. It was expected to last for ten years and have a scrap value of $10,000. The business depreciates non-current assets at 20% on the reducing balance basis. The item of plant was sold on 1 April 20X4 for sale proceeds of $70,000. It is Smart's policy to charge a full year of depreciation in the year of purchase and none in the year of disposal. Smart has an accounting year end of 31 December.

What was the profit on disposal on this asset?

$ [   ]

162 Martin purchased an item of plant at a cost of $100,000 in 1 January 20X2. It was expected to last for six years and had an estimated scrap value of $10,000 at the end of that time. The business depreciates non-current assets on a straight-line basis, with a proportionate charge in the year of purchase and disposal. Martin has an accounting year end of 31 December. The item of plant subsequently was sold on 1 April 20X4 for sale proceeds of $60,000.

What was the loss on disposal on this asset?

$ [   ]

The following information relates to questions 163 to 167.

A machine which had cost of $20,000 and had accumulated depreciation of $17,200 was sold during 20X7 for $4,800. The total cost of machinery shown in the December 20X6 statement of financial position was $180,000 and the related accumulated depreciation was $92,000. The business uses 10% straight line depreciation on machinery and no depreciation is charged in the year in which an asset is sold.

Note: in the exam, all questions will be independent, and not based on a common scenario.

---

163 **What was the balance on the accumulated depreciation account at 31 December 20X7?**

$ [   ]

164 **What was the profit on disposal of the machine?**

$ [   ]

165 **What was the annual depreciation charge for 20X7?**

$ [   ]

166 **What entries are required to record the sale of the machine in 20X7?**

A   Debit cash account with $4,800, debit the machinery account with $4,800 and credit accumulated depreciation account with $9,600.

B   Debit cash with $4,800, credit machinery with $3,400 and credit accumulated depreciation with $1,400.

C   Debit cash with $4,800, debit accumulated depreciation with $17,200 and credit machinery with $22,000.

D   Debit accumulated depreciation with $17,200, debit cash with $4,800, credit machinery with $20,000 and debit disposal with $20,000.

167 **Which of the following best describes the gain or loss on the disposal of a non-current?**

A   The amount by which management over or under charged depreciation for the asset.

B   The extent to which the asset's underlying value changed during its useful life.

C   The correction of forecasting errors when the asset's useful life and residual values were estimated.

D   The remaining value after depreciation has been taken into account.

168 At 30 September 20X2, the following balances existed in the records of Lambda:

Plant and equipment:

Cost $860,000

Accumulated depreciation $397,000

During the year ended 30 September 20X3, plant with a written down value of $37,000 was sold for $49,000. The plant had originally cost $80,000. Plant purchased during the year cost $180,000. The accounting policy of the business is to charge a full year's depreciation in the year of acquisition of an asset and none in the year of sale, using a rate of 10% on the straight line basis.

What carrying amount should appear in Lambda's statement of financial position at 30 September 20X3 for plant and equipment?

$

169 A business with an accounting year end of 31 October bought a non-current asset on 1 July 20X3 for $126,000.

Depreciation is charged at the rate of 15% per annum on the reducing balance basis. On 30 September 20X7 the asset was sold for $54,800. It is the policy of the business to charge a proportionate amount of depreciation in both the year of acquisition and the year of disposal.

What was the loss on sale of the asset (to the nearest $)?

A $19,792

B $8,603

C $7,674

D $1,106

170 A car was purchased by a business in May 20X1 as follows:

	$
Cost	10,000
Road tax	150
Total	10,150

The business has an accounting year end 31 December. The car was traded in for a replacement vehicle in August 20X5 at an agreed value of $5,000.

It was depreciated at 25% per annum on the reducing-balance method, charging a full year's depreciation in the year of purchase and none in the year of sale.

What was the profit on disposal of the vehicle during the year ended December 20X5?

$

171 A business had non-current assets with a net carrying amount of $200,000 at 1 August 20X2. During the year ended 31 July 20X3, the business sold non-current assets for $25,000 on which it made a loss of $5,000. The depreciation charge for the year was $20,000.

What was the carrying amount of non-current assets at 31 July 20X3?

$

172 A non-current asset costing $12,500 was sold at a book loss of $4,500. Depreciation had been provided using the reducing balance, at 20% per annum since its purchase.

Which of the following correctly describes the sale proceeds and length of time for which the asset had been owned?

	Sale proceeds	Length of ownership
A	Cannot be calculated	Cannot be calculated
B	Cannot be calculated	Two years
C	$8,000	Cannot be calculated
D	$8,000	Two years

173 A machine cost $9,000. It has an expected useful life of 6 years, and an expected residual value of $1,000. It is to be depreciated at 30% per annum on the reducing balance basis.

A full year's depreciation is charged in the year of purchase, with none in the year of sale. During year 4, it is sold for $3,000.

What was the loss on disposal of the machine?

$

174 Don sold a machine for $5,300. The machine had been bought three years previously at a cost of $10,000. At the date of sale accumulated depreciation charges amounted to $4,800.

What was the profit on disposal of the machine?

$

175 Jimi sold a machine which originally cost $14,900. At the date of the sale the accumulated depreciation on the machine was $8,940. The sale proceeds were $7,455.

What was the profit or loss on the sale of the machine?

A   A profit of $1,485

B   A loss of $1,485

C   A loss of $1,495

D   A profit of $1,495

176 **Which of the following should be accounted for as capital expenditure?**

A   The purchase of a car by a car dealer for re-sale

B   The purchase of a delivery van by a business

C   The cost of repairing a delivery van by a business

D   The cost of vehicle insurance by a business

177 A machine was purchased for $18,000 on 1 April 20X1 and has been depreciated at 20% each year straight line, assuming no residual value. The depreciation policy of the business is to charge a full year's depreciation in the year of purchase and no depreciation in the year of sale. The car was traded in for a replacement vehicle on 1 August 20X4 for an agreed figure of $8,000.

What was the profit or loss on the disposal of the vehicle for the year ended 31 December 20X4?

A   Profit $800

B   Profit $2,800

C   Profit $4,400

D   Profit $7,200

178 Information relating to two asset disposal transactions was as follows:

	Cost	Accumulated Depreciation	Disposal proceeds
	$	$	$
Asset 1	15,000	8,500	7,500
Asset 2	17,000	9,500	6,500

For each disposal transaction, was there a profit or loss on disposal?

	Profit on disposal	Loss on disposal
Asset 1	*1 0 0 0*	
Asset 2		*✓*

ACCRUALS AND PREPAYMENTS

179 Troy, a property business, received cash totalling $838,600 from tenants during the year ended 31 December 20X6.

Figures for rent in advance and in arrears at the beginning and end of the year were:

	31 December 20X5	31 December 20X6
	$	$
Rent received in advance	102,600	88,700
Rent in arrears (all subsequently received)	42,300	48,400

What amount should be included in Troy's statement of profit or loss for the year ended 31 December 20X6 for rental income?

$ *858600*

180 Details of Bartlett's insurance policy are shown below:

Premium for year ended 31 March 20X6 paid April 20X5	$10,800
Premium for year ending 31 March 20X7 paid April 20X6	$12,000

What figures should be included in the Bartlett's financial statements for the year ended 30 June 20X6?

		Statement of profit or loss $	Statement of financial position $
A		11,100	9,000 prepayment
B		11,700	9,000 prepayment
C		11,100	9,000 accrual
D		11,700	9,000 accrual

181 Vine sublets part of its office accommodation. The rent is received quarterly in advance on 1 January, 1 April, 1 July and 1 October. The annual rent has been $24,000 for some years, but it was increased to $30,000 from 1 July 20X5.

What amounts for rent should appear in Vine's financial statements for the year ended 31 January 20X6?

		Statement of profit or loss $	Statement of financial position $
A		27,500	5,000 accrued income
B		27,000	2,500 accrued income
C		27,000	2,500 prepaid income
D		27,500	5,000 prepaid income

182 At 1 September, the motor expenses account showed 4 months' insurance prepaid of $80 and petrol accrued of $95. During September, the outstanding petrol bill is paid, plus further bills of $245. At 30 September there is a further outstanding petrol bill of $120.

What amount should be shown in the statement of profit or loss for motor expenses for the month of September?

$

183 On 1 May 20X0, A pays a rent bill of $1,800 for the period to 30 April 20X1.

What is the charge to the statement of profit or loss and the entry in the statement of financial position for the year ended 30 November 20X0?

A $1,050 charge to statement of profit or loss and prepayment of $750 in the statement of financial position.

B $1,050 charge to statement of profit or loss and accrual of $750 in the statement of financial position.

C $1,800 charge to statement of profit or loss and no entry in the statement of financial position.

D $750 charge to statement of profit or loss and prepayment of $1,050 in the statement of financial position.

184 The electricity account for the year ended 30 June 20X3 was as follows:

	$
Opening balance for electricity accrued at 1 July 20X2	300
Payments made during the year:	
1 August 20X2 for three months to 31 July 20X2	600
1 November 20X2 for three months to 31 October 20X2	720
1 February 20X3 for three months to 31 January 20X3	900
30 June 20X3 for three months to 30 April 20X3	840

Which of the following is the appropriate entry for electricity?

	Accrued at June 20X3	Charged to statement of profit or loss, year ended 30 June 20X3
A	$Nil	$3,060
B	$460	$3,320
C	$560	$3,320
D	$560	$3,420

185 Farthing's year-end is 30 September. On 1 January 20X6 the organisation took out a loan of $100,000 with annual interest of 12%. The interest is payable in equal instalments on the first day of April, July, October and January in arrears.

How much should be charged to the statement of profit or loss account for the year ended 30 September 20X6, and how much should be accrued on the statement of financial position?

	Statement of profit or loss	Statement of financial position
A	$12,000	$3,000
B	$9,000	$3,000
C	$9,000	Nil
D	$6,000	$3,000

186 On the 1 January 20X8, a business had prepaid insurance of $10,000. On 1 August 20X8, it paid, in full, the annual insurance invoice of $36,000, to cover the following year.

What is the amount charged in the statement of profit or loss and the amount shown in the statement of financial position at 31 December 20X8?

	Statement of profit or loss	Statement of financial position
	$	$
A	5,000	24,000
B	22,000	23,000
C	25,000	21,000
D	36,000	15,000

187 **Which of the following statements is correct?**

A   Accruals decrease profit

B   Accrued income decreases profit

C   A prepayment is a liability

D   An accrual is an asset

188 Flavia's year-end is 31 March. On 1 January 20X3 she took out a loan of $250,000 with annual interest of 10%. The interest is payable in equal instalments on the first day of April, July, October and January in arrears.

How much should be charged to the statement of profit or loss account for the year ended 31 March 20X3, and how much should be accrued on the statement of financial position?

	Statement of profit or loss	Statement of financial position
A	$25,000	$18,750
B	$6,250	$6,250
C	$6,250	Nil
D	$18,750	6,250

189 On 23 May 20X7, Julie used cash to pay the rent on her business premises for the three months to 31 August 20X7 in advance.

On 23 May, how is Julie's accusing equation affected by this transaction?

	Assets	Liabilities	Capital
A	Unchanged	Unchanged	Unchanged
B	Unchanged	Reduced	Reduced
C	Reduced	Unchanged	Unchanged
D	Reduced	Unchanged	Reduced

190 In September 20X6 Alison paid $7,800 for rent for the four months from 1 October 20X6.

What should be reported on Alison's statement of financial position at 30 November 20X6?

A   An accrual of $3,900

B   An accrual of $1,950

C   A prepayment of $3,900

D   A prepayment of $1,950

191 In the year to 30 November 20X6 Norah paid $1,765 for electricity. At 1 December 20X5 she had an accrual of $264 for electricity. At 30 November 20X6 the accrual was $312.

What is the charge for electricity in Norah's statement of profit or loss for the year to 30 November 20X6?

$\boxed{\text{\$}\qquad\qquad\qquad}$

192 When he closed his ledger accounts at 30 April 20X7 Luther's wages expense account had a debit balance of $87,963. Luther also had to make an accrual of $1,268 for outstanding wages.

What is Luther's opening credit balance for wages at 1 May 20X7?

$\boxed{\text{\$}\qquad\qquad\qquad}$

193 The rent account for a business was as follows:

Rent

		$			$
1/1/X5	Bal b/d	1,000			
1/2/X5	Bank	3,000			
1/5/X5	Bank	3,000			
1/8/X5	Bank	3,600	31/12/X5	Profit or loss	13,000
1/11/X5	Bank	3,600	31/12/X5	Bal c/d	1,200
		14,200			14,200
1/1/X6	Bal b/d	1,200			

Which of the following best describes the rent expense?

A   Cash paid $13,000   Charge for year $13,200

B   Cash paid $13,000   Charge for year $13,000

C   Cash paid $13,200   Charge for year $13,000

D   Cash paid $13,200   Charge for year $13,200

194 A business compiling its accounts for the year to 31 January each year, pays rent quarterly in advance on 1 January, 1 April, 1 July and 1 October each year. After remaining unchanged for some years, the rent was increased from $24,000 per year to $30,000 per year as from 1 July 20X3.

What is the rent expense that should appear in the statement of profit or loss for the year ended 31 January 20X4?

A $30,000

B $27,000

C $27,500

D $24,000

195 **On 1 May 20X3, Blister pays a rent bill of $1,800 for the period to 30 April 20X4. What is the charge to the statement of profit or loss and the entry in the statement of financial position for the year ended 30 November 20X3?**

A $1,050 charge to profit or loss and prepayment of $750 in the statement of financial position

B $1,050 charge to profit or loss and accrual of $750 in the statement of financial position

C $1,800 charge to profit or loss and no entry in the statement of financial position

D $750 charge to profit or loss and prepayment of $1,050 in the statement of financial position

196 **On 1 June 20X2, H paid an insurance invoice of $2,400 for the year to 31 May 20X3. What is the charge to the statement of profit or loss and the entry in the statement of financial position for the year ended 31 December 20X2?**

A $1,000 profit or loss and prepayment of $1,400

B $1,400 profit or loss and accrual of $1,000

C $1,400 profit or loss and prepayment of $1,000

D $2,400 profit or loss and no entry in the statement of financial position

197 At 31 March 20X3, accrued rent payable was $300. During the year ended 31 March 20X4, rent paid was $4,000, including an invoice for $1,200 for the quarter ended 30 April 20X4.

What was the charge to profit or loss for rent payable for the year ended 31 March 20X4?

$ _____

198 The electricity account for the year ended 30 June 20X3 was as follows:

	$
Opening balance for electricity accrued at 1 July 20X2	300
Payments made during the year:	
1 August 20X2 for three months to 31 July 20X2	600
1 November 20X2 for three months to 31 October 20X2	720
1 February 20X3 for three months to 31 January 20X3	900
30 June 20X3 for three months to 30 April 20X3	840

Which of the following are the appropriate entries for electricity?

	Accrued at June 20X3	Charged to profit or loss year ended 30 June 20X3
A	$Nil	$3,060
B	$460	$3,320
C	$560	$3,320
D	$560	$3,420

199 The annual insurance premium for S for the period 1 July 20X3 to 30 June 20X4 was $13,200, which was 10% more than the previous year. Insurance premiums are paid on 1 July.

What was the profit or loss charge for insurance for the year ended 31 December 20X3?

$ [   ]

200 Arlene has paid $5,520 for rent for the six-month period to 31 August 20X1.

What prepayment is required when preparing accounts for the year ended 30 June 20X1?

$ [   ]

201 The last electricity bill received by Graham was for the three-month period to 30 September 20X1. This bill was for $2,100.

What accrual is required when preparing the accounts for the year to 30 November 20X1?

$ [   ]

202 Jennifer is preparing her year-end accounts and she has to deal with a prepayment for rent.

Which of the following statements is correct?

A   The prepayment will increase the charge to profit or loss

B   The prepayment will reduce the charge to profit or loss

C   The prepayment has no effect on profit or loss

D   The prepayment will only affect profit or loss

203 When he prepared his draft accounts, Ralph included $1,400 as an accrual for rent for two months. However he should have provided for only one month's rent.

How will Ralph's current liabilities be affected when he adjusts the accrual?

A   Reduced by $1,400

B   Increased by $1,400

C   Reduced by $700

D   Increased by $700

204 Beth's draft accounts for the year to 31 October 20X5 report a loss of $1,486. When she prepared the accounts, Beth did not include an accrual of $1,625 and a prepayment of $834.

What is Beth's profit or loss for the year to 31 October 20X5 following the inclusion of the accrual and prepayment?

A   A loss of $695

B   A loss of $2,277

C   A loss of $3,945

D   A profit of $1,807

205 Dave Hull is preparing his final accounts for the year to 30 April 20X6. The last payment Dave made for electricity was in March 20X6 when he paid $3,270 for the three months to 28 February 20X6.

What adjustment does Dave need to make when preparing his final accounts for the year to 30 April 20X6?

A   A prepayment of $1,090

B   An accrual of $1,090

C   A prepayment of $2,180

D   An accrual of $2,180

206 In Theo's statement of profit or loss for the year ended 31 May 20X6 the charge for motor repairs was $2,850. This included an accrual of $220.

When Theo's opening trial balance at 1 June 20X6 is prepared, what is the correct balance on the motor repairs account?

A $220 (debit)

B $220 (credit)

C $2,850 (debit)

D $2,850 (credit)

207 Information relating to two expenses was as follows:

	Opening accrual	Cash paid	P&L expense
	$	$	$
Repairs and renewals	2,000	39,500	36,500
Light and heat	1,000	25,000	25,500

For each transaction, was there an accrual or prepayment at the end of the accounting period?

	Accrual	Prepayment
Repairs and renewals		
Light and heat		

IRRECOVERABLE DEBTS AND ALLOWANCES FOR RECEIVABLES

208 Newell's receivables' ledger control account shows a balance at the end of the year of $58,200 before making the following adjustments:

(i) Newell wishes to write off debts amounting to $8,900 as he believes that they are irrecoverable.

(ii) He also wishes to make an allowance for Carroll's debt of $1,350 and Juff's debt of $750.

Newell's allowance for receivables at the last year end was $5,650.

What is the total charge to the statement of profit or loss in respect of the above?

$

209 In the statement of financial position at 31 December 20X5, Boris reported net receivables of $12,000. During 20X6 he made sales on credit of $125,000 and received cash from credit customers amounting to $115,500. At 31 December 20X6, Boris wished to write off debts of $7,100 and increase the allowance for receivables by $950 to $2,100.

What is the net receivables figure to include in the statement of financial position at 31 December 20X6?

$

210 At 1 July 20X5, Arthur's allowance for receivables was $48,000. At 30 June 20X6, trade receivables amounted to $838,000. It was decided to write off $72,000 of these debts and adjust the allowance for receivables to $60,000.

What are the final amounts for inclusion in Arthur's statement of financial position at 30 June 20X6?

	Trade receivables	Allowance for receivables	Net balance
	$	$	$
A	838,000	60,000	778,000
B	766,000	60,000	706,000
C	766,000	108,000	658,000
D	838,000	108,000	730,000

211 In the year ended 30 September 20X8, Fauntleroy had sales of $7,000,000. Year-end receivables amounted to 5% of annual sales. At 1 October 20X7, the allowance for receivables was $11,667 and this should be increased to $14,000 at 30 September 20X8.

During the year ended 30 September 20X8, irrecoverable debts amounting to $3,200 were written off and debts amounting to $450 which had been written off previously were recovered.

What is the irrecoverable debt expense for the year?

$

212 On 1 January 20X3 Tipton's trade receivables were $10,000. The following information relates to the year ended 31 December 20X3:

	$
Credit sales	100,000
Cash receipts	90,000
Irrecoverable debts written off in year	800
Discounts received	700

Cash receipts include $1,000 in respect of a receivable previously written off.

What was the carrying amount of receivables at 31 December 20X3?

$ 20 400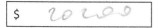

213 A business has been notified that a customer who owed $500 has been declared insolvent. The business had previously made an allowance against this receivable.

What accounting entries are required to account for the amount due from the insolvent customer?

	Debit	*Credit*
A	Irrecoverable debts account	Receivables' ledger control account
B	Receivables' ledger control account	Irrecoverable debts account
C	Allowance for receivables account	Receivables' ledger control account
D	Receivables' ledger control account	Allowance for receivables account

214 Headington was owed $37,500 by its customers at 1 January 20X8 and $49,000 at 31 December 20X8.

During the year, cash sales of $263,500 and credit sales of $357,500 were made, contras with the payables ledger control account amounted to $1,750 and discounts received totalled $21,400. Irrecoverable debts of $3,500 were written off and Headington wishes to increase its allowance for receivables from $7,500 to $10,000.

What was the cash received from receivables during the year ended 31 December 20X8?

$ 340 750

215 Alex had total receivables of $87,000 and an allowance for receivables of $2,500 at the start of the accounting year.

During the year, two specific debts were written off, one for $800 and the other for $550. A debt of $350 that had been written off as irrecoverable in the previous year was paid during the year. At the year-end, total receivables were $90,000 and the allowance for receivables was $2,300.

What was the charge to the statement of profit or loss for the year in relating to irrecoverable debts and the change in the allowance for receivables?

$ 800

216 What is the effect of an increase in the allowance for receivables?

A It will result in an increase in net current assets

B It will result in a decrease in net current assets

C It will result in an increase in sales

D It will result in a decrease in drawings

217 At 31 December 20X7, Chester's receivables' balance was $230,000. He wishes to make specific allowance for Emily's debt of $450, Lulu's debt of $980 and Sandy's debt of $5,000.

What amount should be credited to the statement of profit or loss relating to the allowance for receivables if the allowance at 1 January 20X7 was $11,700?

$ _____

218 At 31 March 20X9 Sally was owed $47,744 by her customers. At the same date her allowance for receivables was $3,500.

How should these balances be reported on Sally's statement of financial position at 31 March 20X9?

A $44,244 as a current asset

B $3,500 as a current asset and $47,744 as a current liability

C $47,744 as a current asset and $3,500 as a current liability

D $51,244 as a current asset

219 The allowance for receivables in the ledger of Bertie at 31 October 20X1 was $9,000. During the year ended 31 October 20X2, irrecoverable debts of $5,000 were written off.

Accounts receivable balances at 31 October 20X2 were $120,000 and, based upon a review of receivables at that date, the allowance for receivables required was $6,000.

What was the total charge for irrecoverable and debts and change in allowance for receivables in the statement of profit or loss for the year ended 31 October 20X2?

$ _____

220 At 1 November 20X4 Dorothy's receivables allowance was $5,670. At 31 October 20X5 she was owed $275,600 by her customers. Following a review of receivables Dorothy has determined that an allowance of $5,512 is required at 31 October 20X5.

What amount should be credited in Dorothy's statement of profit or loss for the year ended 31 October 20X5 relating to the change in the allowance for receivables?

$ _____

CAPITAL AND FINANCE COSTS

221 Tommy started a business and paid $15,000 into the business bank account. Tommy also obtained a bank loan of $5,000 to help finance the business.

How should be two transactions be classified in the statement of financial position?

A   Proprietor's capital of $20,000

B   Business liabilities of $20,000

C   Proprietor's capital of $5,000 and a business liability of $15,000

D   Proprietor's capital of $15,000 and a business liability of $5,000

222 A sole trader had opening capital of $12,000 and closing capital of $14,500. During the period, the owner introduced capital of $1,500 and withdrew $6,000 for her own use.

What was the profit for the period?

$

223 A sole trader had opening capital of $12,000 and closing capital of $14,500. During the period, the owner made a loss of $13,000 withdrew $7,500 for his own use.

What was capital introduced into the business during the year?

$

224 Paul, a sole trader, had an opening capital balance of $23,000. During the accounting year, he made a loss of $2,500. In addition, he introduced capital of 3,000 and made drawings of $8,200.

What was the capital account balance at the end of the accounting period?

$

225 Callum, a sole trader, had an opening capital balance of $35,000. During the accounting year, he made drawings of $14,600. At the end of the accounting year, Callum's capital account balance was $30,000.

What was Callum's profit for the year?

$

226 Rosie, a sole trader, had a closing capital balance of $42,500. During the accounting year, she made drawings of $15,700 and introduced capital of $2,750. Rosie made a profit for the year of $13,800.

What was Rosie's capital account balance at the start of the accounting year?

$

227 Andrew works as a handyman and joiner. At 1 July 20X5 he had a capital account balance of $12,735. During the year, he made withdrawals from the business for his own use of $2,345, and had a capital account balance of $2,690 at 30 June 20X6.

What was Andrew's loss for the year ended 30 June 20X6?

$ ⬚

228 On 1 July 20X5 Lucas introduced capital of $7,500 into his business and also raised a loan from the bank for the same amount at an interest rate of 8% per annum, payable annually in arrears.

How should this information be classified in the statement of financial position at 31 December 20X5?

A   Business liabilities of $15,300

B   Proprietor's capital of $7,500 and business liabilities of $7,500

C   Proprietor's capital of $7,500 and business liabilities of $7,800

D   Proprietor's capital of $15,000

229 Ella, a sole trader, had an opening capital balance of $28,350 and a closing capital balance of $25,685. In addition, Ella made a profit for the year of $9,335 and introduced capital of $3,000.

What were Ella's drawings from the business for the year?

$ ⬚

230 Daniel had opening capital of $18,500 and closing capital of $16,750. During the year, he made a loss of $8,000 withdrew $8,500 for his own use.

How much capital did Daniel introduce during the year?

$ ⬚

231 **What is the correct accounting treatment of finance costs accrued on a loan taken out by Michelle during the year?**

A   Debit: Drawings, and   Credit: Capital

B   Debit: Capital, and   Credit: Profit or loss

C   Debit: Profit or loss, and   Credit: Liabilities

D   Debit: Profit or loss, and   Credit: Bank

CONTROL ACCOUNTS, RECONCILIATIONS AND ERRORS

232 After completing his final accounts, Kevin found that he had understated a prepayment.

How are Kevin's net profit and capital affected by correction of this error?

	Net profit	Capital
A	Increased	Increased
B	Increased	Decreased
C	Decreased	Increased
D	Decreased	Decreased

233 Elaine is preparing her bank reconciliation. She has noted the following:

(i)   the bank has levied charges on her account

(ii)   a cheque payable to S. Wright has not been presented at the bank.

Which of the above errors require an entry in the bank account in her general ledger?

A   both (i) and (ii)

B   (i) only

C   neither (i) nor (ii)

D   (ii) only

234 When entering invoices in the purchase day book, Elaine recorded an invoice for $126 for motor expenses as $162. The day book totals have been posted to the general ledger.

What accounting entries are required to correct this error?

	Debit		Credit	
	$		$	
A	36	Motor expenses	36	Payables' control
B	36	Payables' ledger control	36	Motor expenses
C	288	Motor expenses	288	Payables' control
D	288	Payables' ledger control	288	Motor expenses

235 Patrick is preparing a reconciliation between the total of the list of balances from his receivables ledger, which is $37,552, and the balance on the receivables control account in his general ledger, which is $38,842.

He found that the following errors have been made:

(i)   a debit balance of $1,200 was omitted from the list of balances

(ii)   a credit note for $375 was recorded in the daybook as an invoice; and

(iii) the total of the sales invoices in the sales daybook was overstated by $90.

What value should be reported in Patrick's statement of financial position for receivables?

$ [   ]

236 Carol has prepared the following reconciliation of the balance on the payables' ledger control account in her general ledger with the list of balances on the payables' ledger:

	$
Total of list of balances	86,579
Balance omitted from list	1,385
	————
Balance on control account	87,964
	————

What should be reported in Carol's statement of financial position for trade payables?

A   A current asset of $86,579

B   A current liability of $86,579

C   A current asset of $87,964

D   A current liability of $87,964

The following information relates to questions 237 and 238.

While carrying out the reconciliation of the balance on the payables control account in the general ledger with the list of balances from the payables ledger, Celine discovered the following errors:

(i)   A payment of $1,700 in full settlement of a balance of $1,714 was correctly recorded on the supplier's account, but only $1,700 was posted to the control account.

(ii)   The total of the purchase day book was understated by $900.

(iii)   A supplier's credit note was incorrectly recorded in the day book as an invoice.

(iv)   No entries were made to record an arrangement to offset a balance of $620 against a balance in the receivables ledger.

Note: in the exam, all questions will be independent, and not based on a common scenario.

---

237   Which of the above errors require a correcting entry in the general ledger?

A   (i) and (ii) only

B   (ii) and (iii) only

C   (iii) and (iv) only

D   (i), (ii), (iii) and (iv)

238   Which of the above errors should be dealt with as an adjustment to the list of balances from the suppliers' ledger?

A   (i) and (ii) only

B   (ii) and (iii) only

C   (iii) and (iv) only

D   (i), (ii), (iii) and (iv)

239 Consider the following two statements relating to control accounts.

Is each statement true or false?

	True	False
Control accounts can help to speed up the preparation of draft accounts by providing the statement of financial position values for trade receivables and trade payables	✓	
Control accounts are always used in double entry bookkeeping		✓

The following information relates to questions 240 and 241.

Jamie is preparing a reconciliation of the balance on the payables ledger control account in the general ledger to the total of the list of balances on the accounts in the payables ledger. He has discovered the following:

(i)   a debit balance on a supplier's account was listed as a credit balance

(ii)   an invoice for $378 was entered in the purchase day book as $387.

Note: in the exam, all questions will be independent, and not based on a common scenario.

240 **Which of the errors will require an adjustment to the payables ledger control account in the general ledger?**

A   Neither (i) nor (ii)

B   (i) only

C   (ii) only

D   Both (i) and (ii)

241 **Which of the errors will require an adjustment to the list of balances?**

A   Neither (i) nor (ii)

B   (i) only

C   (ii) only

D   Both (i) and (ii)

242 Shirley has prepared the following reconciliation of the balance on the receivables' ledger control account in her general ledger to the total of the list of receivables' ledger balances:

	$
Balance on general ledger control account	35,776
Less: Balance omitted from list of balances	452
	35,324
Add: Sales day book undercast	900
Total of list of balances	36,224

What is the correct receivables' ledger control account balance to be reported on the statement of financial position?

$ [   ]

243 When Yvonne checked the entries in her cash book with her bank statement seven cheques with a total value of $3,259 had not been presented at her bank. Yvonne had instructed her bank to cancel two of these cheques, but did not make any entries in her cash book. The value of the cancelled cheques is $642.

What entry should Yvonne make in the bank account in her general ledger to correct the balance?

A   Debit $642

B   Debit $2,617

C   Credit $642

D   Credit $2,617

244 When the totals from the purchases day book were posted to the general ledger, $650 for stationery was posted to the wrong side of the stationery account.

Which of the following will correct the error on the stationery account?

A   A debit entry of $650

B   A debit entry of $1,300

C   A credit entry of $650

D   A credit entry of $650

245 Consider the following statements relating to suspense accounts:

Is each statement true or false?

	True	*False*
A separate suspense account should be opened for each error in the ledgers		
A suspense account is sometimes opened to complete postings whilst more information is sought on a transaction		

246 Norma's trial balance includes a suspense account with a credit balance of $280. She has discovered that a supplier's invoice for $140 was entered twice in the purchase day book.

What is the balance on the suspense account after the error is corrected?

A   Nil

B $140 credit

C $280 credit

D $420 credit

247 The total of the balances on the individual suppliers' accounts in Arnold's payables ledger is $81,649. The balance on the payables control account in his general ledger is $76,961. He has discovered that an invoice for $4,688 has been posted twice to the correct supplier's account and that payments totalling $1,606 which he made by standing order have been omitted from his records.

What amount should be reported in Arnold's statement of financial position for trade payables?

$ [   ]

248 Jenny has recorded the following journal entry:

Debit   Purchases $1,500

Credit   Stationery $1,500

What is the correct narrative for Jenny's journal entry?

A   Being cash purchase of stationery

B   Being credit purchase of stationery

C   Being correction of error – purchases originally recorded as stationery

D   Being correction of error – stationery originally recorded as purchases

The following information relates to questions 249 and 250.

The accounts payable ledger clerk of Q Co extracted a listing of balances due on 31 July 20X0. These were totalled and found to equal $176,000. The balance on the trade payables control account as at the same date was $179,000. Q Co's chief accountant called for an investigation and uncovered several errors.

Note: in the exam, all questions will be independent, and not based on a common scenario.

249 Q Co's purchase day book was overcast by $4,000 during July 20X0.

Which of the following adjustments would correct this error?

A   Debit the trade payables control account and credit purchases and sales tax.

B   Credit the trade payables control account and debit purchases and sales tax.

C   Reduce the balance on an individual payable account and reduce the total for all balances.

D   Increase the balance on an individual payable account and increase the total for all balances.

250 H's account in Q Co's purchase ledger had been miscast and the total due overstated by $1,000.

Which of the following adjustments would correct this error?

A   Debit the accounts payable control account and credit purchases and sales tax.

B   Credit the accounts payable control account and debit purchases and sales tax.

C   Reduce the balance on an individual supplier's account and reduce the total for all balances.

D   Increase the balance on an individual supplier's account and increase the total for all balances.

251 S Co received discounts of 2,700 for prompt payments made during July. An oversight meant that this information was not passed on to either the general ledger or the payables ledger clerks.

Which of the following adjustments would correct this error?

A   Debit the accounts payable control account and credit discounts received. Leave the purchase ledger total unadjusted.

B   Credit the accounts payable control account and debit discounts received. Leave the purchase ledger total unadjusted.

C   Reduce the balance on the individual supplier accounts and reduce the total for all balances. Leave the accounts payable control unadjusted.

D   Reduce the balance on the individual payables ledger account and therefore also reduce the total of payables ledger balances. Debit the accounts payable control account and credit discounts received in the general ledger.

252 The following attempt at a bank reconciliation statement has been prepared by T Co:

	$
Overdraft per bank statement	38,600
Add: deposits not credited	41,200
	————
	79,800
Less: outstanding cheques	3,300
	————
Overdraft per cash book	$76,500
	————

Assuming that the bank statement balance of $38,600 was correct, what was the correct credit balance per the cash book?

$

253 **After checking a business cash book against the bank statement, which TWO of the following four items could require an entry in the cash book?**

	Selected answer
Bank charges	
Cheque not presented	
A dishonoured cheque from a customer	
Deposits not credited	

254 **Which of the following statements best explains the imprest system of petty cash control?**

A   Weekly expenditure cannot exceed a set amount

B   The exact amount of expenditure is reimbursed at intervals to maintain a fixed float

C   All expenditure out of the petty cash must be properly authorised

D   Regular equal amounts of cash are transferred into petty cash at intervals

255 The purchases day book of Arbroath has been undercast by $500, and the sales day book has been overcast by $700. Arbroath maintains payables and receivables ledger control accounts as part of the double entry bookkeeping system.

How will the errors be corrected and what will be their effect?

A   Make adjustments to the ledger balances of the individual receivables and payables, with no effect on profit

B   Make adjustments to the ledger balances of the individual receivables and payables, with a decrease in profit of $1,200

C   Make adjustments to the control accounts, with no effect on profit

D   Make adjustments to the control accounts, with a decrease in profit of $1,200

256 In reconciling the accounts receivable ledger control account with the list of receivable ledger balances of Snooks, the following errors were found:

1   The sales receivables day book had been overcast by $370.

2   A total of $940 from the cash receipts book had been recorded in the accounts receivable ledger control account as $490.

What adjustments must be made to correct the errors?

A   Credit accounts receivable control account $820. Decrease total of sales ledger balances by $820.

B   Credit accounts receivable control account $820. No change in total of sales ledger balances.

C   Debit accounts receivable control account $80. No change in total of sales ledger balances.

D   Debit accounts receivable control account $80. Increase total of sales ledger balances by $80.

257 For the month of November 20X0 Figgin's purchases totalled $225,600 with sales tax of $39,480. The total of $265,080 has been credited to the accounts payable ledger control account as $260,580.

Which of the following adjustments is correct?

	Control account	List of payables balances
A	$4,500 Cr	No adjustment
B	$4,500 Cr	Increase by $4,500
C	$29,340 Dr	No effect
D	$33,840 Dr	Increase by $4,500

258 A supplier sends you a statement showing a balance outstanding of $14,350. Your own records show a balance outstanding of $14,500.

What could be a possible reason for this situation?

A   The supplier sent an invoice for $150 which you have not yet received

B   The supplier has allowed you $150 cash discount which you had omitted to enter in your general ledger

C   You have paid the supplier $150 which he has not yet accounted for

D   You have returned goods worth $150 which the supplier has not yet accounted for

259 The receivables ledger control account at 1 May had balances of $32,750 debit and $1,275 credit. During May, sales of $125,000 were made on credit. Receipts from credit customers amounted to $122,500 and contras with the payables ledger control account amounted to $550. Credit customers returned goods totalling $1,300, for which credit notes were issued.

What were the receivables ledger control account balances at 31 May?

A $35,125 debit and $3,000 credit

B $35,675 debit and $2,500 credit

C $36,725 debit and $2,000 credit

D $36,725 debit and $1,000 credit

260 **Which of the following statements is/are correct?**

(i)   The receivables ledger control account balance must be correct if it agrees with the total of the list of balances from the receivables ledger.

(ii)   If there is a difference between the balance on the receivables ledger control account and the total of the list of balances from the receivables ledger, the balance on the control account is always correct.

A   Both (i) and (ii)

B   Neither (i) nor (ii)

C   (i) only

D   (ii) only

261 Arlene posted an invoice for motor vehicle repairs of $240 to the building repairs account.

What journal entry is required to correct this error?

	Debit	*Credit*
A	Equipment repairs	Building repairs

Being correction of an error of omission – invoice posted to wrong account

B	Building repairs	Equipment repairs

Being correction of an error of omission – invoice posted to wrong account

C	Building repairs	Equipment repairs

Being correction of an error of commission – invoice posted to wrong account

D	Equipment repairs	Building repairs

Being correction of an error of commission – invoice posted to wrong account

262 One of Brian's customers has returned goods valued at $670. The goods had been sold on credit.

What general ledger journal entries should be made to record the return of goods?

	Debit	*Credit*
A	Receivables' ledger control account	Bank

Being return of goods

B	Bank	Receivables' ledger control account

Being return of goods

C	Receivables' ledger control account	Sales returns

Being return of goods

D	Sales returns	Receivables' ledger control account

Being return of goods

263 Tony made one error when he posted the total value of invoices from the purchase day book to the general ledger. He posted $274,865 to the debit side of the purchases account. The correct total was $274,685.

How is the trial balance affected by this error?

A   The total of the debit balances and the total of the credit balances will agree, but will be overstated

B   The total of the debit balances and the total of the credit balances will agree, but will be understated

C   The total of the debit balances will exceed the total of the credit balances

D   The total of the credit balances will exceed the total of the debit balances

264 Linda found the following when carrying out her bank reconciliation:

(i)   a cheque for $7,523 has not been presented at the bank

(ii)   a cheque for $560 has been incorrectly recorded as $650 in Linda's ledger.

Which of these items will require an entry in Linda's general ledger?

A   (i) only

B   (ii) only

C   Both (i) and (ii)

D   Neither (i) nor (ii)

265 Trevor's trial balance includes a suspense account with a debit balance of $900. He has discovered that:

(i)   a supplier's invoice for $16,700 was posted to the correct side of the purchases account as $17,600 (the correct entry was posted to the payables control account); and

(ii)   a cheque for $900 has not been recorded in his ledger.

What was the balance on the suspense account after these errors are corrected?

A   Nil

B $900

C $1,800

D $2,700

266 Gayle paid for office cleaning in cash. She made the following entries in her general ledger:

Debit   Trade payables

Credit   Office cleaning expenses

Which accounts require a correcting entry?

A   Office cleaning expenses and cash only

B   Office cleaning expenses and trade payables only

C   Cash and trade payables only

D   Office cleaning expenses, cash and trade payables

267 Tony's bookkeeper has prepared the following trade payables' ledger reconciliation:

Balance on payables' ledger control account	$78,553
Less: Discount not recorded in general ledger	$128
	————
	$78,425
Add: Debit balance of $100 included in list of balances as credit balance	$200
	————
Total of list of balances	$78,625

What is the correct payables' ledger control account balance to be reported in the statement of financial position?

$

268 Jodie is carrying out a reconciliation of the bank account in her general ledger with the balance on her bank statement.

She has found the following reasons for the difference between the two balances:

(i)   Some cheques paid to suppliers have not been presented at the bank.

(ii)   The bank has made charges on Jodie's account.

(iii)   A customer has paid $980 directly into Jodie's bank account.

Which of the above items will require an entry in the general ledger?

A   (i) and (ii) only

B   (ii) and (iii) only

C   (i) and (iii) only

D   (i), (ii) and (iii)

269 You are preparing a client's final accounts. You know that the client's bookkeeper has correctly completed a reconciliation of the bank balance in the general ledger to the balance on the bank statement. The balances from the general ledger and the bank statement were:

General ledger balance $2,358 (credit)   Bank statement balance $1,053 (debit)

The difference between the two balances is explained by unpresented cheques and outstanding lodgements.

How should the bank balance be reported in the final accounts?

A   As a current asset of $1,053

B   As a current liability of $1,053

C   As a current asset of $2,358

D   As a current liability of $2,358

270 Jody knows that a number of errors were made when her day books were posted to the general ledger.

Which of the following errors will be detected when a trial balance is extracted?

(i)   Error of transposition

(ii)   Error of commission

(iii)   Error of complete omission

(iv)   Error of single entry

A   (i) and (ii)

B   (ii) and (iii)

C   (iii) and (iv)

D   (i) and (iv)

271 A sales invoice for $3,450 was recorded in Susan's general ledger as follows:

Debit   Revenue $3,540

Credit   Trade receivables $3,540

If the errors are not corrected before the final accounts are drafted, how will Susan's net profit for the year be affected?

A   Understated by $90

B   Overstated by $90

C   Understated by $6,990

D   Overstated by $6990

272 In the year to 31 October 20X6, Nadine recorded some revenue expenditure as capital expenditure.

What is the effect on Nadine's profit for the year ended 31 October 20X6 and her net assets at that date?

	Profit	Net assets
A	Overstated	Overstated
B	Overstated	Understated
C	Understated	Overstated
D	Understated	Understated

273 When Pete's trial balance was extracted, the total of the debit balances was $420 less than the total of the credit balances. He opened a suspense account while he checked the entries. He then found that:

(i) a cash sale for $80 was entered correctly in the cash account, but no entry was made in the sales account

(ii) when journal entries were posted to the general ledger, a debit entry of $100 was incorrectly recorded as a credit entry of $700.

When Pete corrects these errors what is the balance on his suspense account?

A $300 credit

B $460 credit

C $1,140 debit

D $1,300 debit

274 Jane prepared her bank reconciliation. The cash book balance in her general ledger was $422 credit. The only items which needed to be dealt with were:

(i) a cheque for $822 issued to a supplier which has not yet appeared on the bank statement

(ii) interest received of $153 which was credited by the bank, but not recorded by Jane.

What was the closing balance on Jane's bank statement?

A $269 overdrawn

B $1,091 overdrawn

C $553 cash at bank

D $1,197 cash at bank

275 At 30 April 20X8 the balance on the bank account in Jim's general ledger showed that he had $685 cash at the bank. When he prepared his bank reconciliation, he found that he had omitted bank charges of $722 for the year to 30 April 20X8.

What cash book balance should be included on Jim's opening trial balance at 1 May 20X8?

A $685 debit

B $685 credit

C $37 debit

D $37 credit

276 Anne has prepared the following reconciliation between the balance on her trade payables' ledger control account in the general ledger and the list of balances from her payables' ledger:

	$
Balance per payables' ledger control account	68,566
Credit balance omitted from list of balances from payables' ledger	(127)
	———
	68,439
Undercasting of purchases day book	99
	———
Total of list of balances	68,538
	———

What balance should be reported on Anne's statement of financial position for trade payables?

$ [   ]

277 Phillip's bank reconciliation statement shows outstanding lodgements paid in by Phillip of $3,800 and outstanding cheques to suppliers of $3,500. His bank account in his ledger shows a debit balance of $25,000.

What balance does Phillip's bank statement show?

A $25,000

B $24,700

C $25,300

D $32,300

278 The following attempt at a bank reconciliation statement has been prepared by Reg:

	$
Overdraft per bank statement	38,600
Add: deposits not credited	41,200
	———
	79,800
Less: outstanding cheques	3,300
	———
Overdraft per cash book	$76,500
	———

Assuming the bank statement balance of $38,600 is correct, what should the cash book balance be?

A $76,500 overdrawn

B $5,900 overdrawn

C $700 overdrawn

D $5,900 cash at bank

279 The balance on the cash account for a business at the end of June was an overdraft of $89.93. At that date there were also unpresented cheques totalling $154.38 and an outstanding deposit of $60.00. It was also discovered that during the month of June the bank had charged the business interest on its overdraft for the previous quarter of $16.45.

What is the correct balance on the cash account at the end of June?

A $73.48 overdrawn

B $106.38 overdrawn

C $167.86 overdrawn

D $200.76 overdrawn

280 A business has a debit balance on its cash book of $148.00 but the bank statement shows a different balance. The following items have also been discovered:

(i)   the bank statement shows that there were bank charges for the period of $10 which have not been recorded in the cash account

(ii)   a standing order payment for $25 has also been mistakenly omitted from the cash account

(iii)   cheques totalling $125 had been written and sent to suppliers but had not yet been presented

(iv)   a cheque for $85 had been paid into the bank but was still outstanding.

What is the balance on the bank statement?

A $73

B $113

C $153

D $223

281 The bank statement shows an overdraft of $210. Uncredited lodgements are $30 and unpresented cheques are $83. A dishonoured cheque for $28 was included on the bank statement but has not yet been written into the cash book.

What is the correct cash book balance?

A $263 overdrawn

B $235 overdrawn

C $157 overdrawn

D $129 overdrawn

282 The bank statement shows a balance at the bank of $1,360, whilst the cash book balance on the same date is $1,250.

How could this discrepancy be explained?

A   Uncredited lodgement of $110

B   Bank charges of $110 not yet recorded in the cash book

C   Bank interest received of $55 credited in the cash book

D   A dishonoured cheque for $55 which the business did not know about until it was returned, after the date of the bank statement

283 Which of the following items would not lead to a difference between the total of the balances on the accounts receivable ledger and the balance on the receivables' ledger control account?

A   An error in totalling the sales day book

B   An error in totalling the receipts column of the cash book

C   An overstatement of an entry in an accounts receivable account

D   An entry posted to the wrong accounts receivable account

284 For the month of November 20X0 Figgins Co made purchases at a cost of $225,600 plus sales tax of $33,840. The total of $259,440 has been credited to the payables' ledger control account as $254,940.

Which of the following adjustments will correct the error?

	Control account	List of payables' balances
A	$4,500 Cr	No adjustment
B	$4,500 Cr	Increase by $4,500
C	$29,340 Dr	No effect
D	$33,840 Dr	Increase by $4,500

285 ANO issued a supplier statement to BNO showing a balance outstanding of $14,350. BNO's records show a balance outstanding of $14,500.

From BNO's perspective, which of the following statements could be a reason that explains this difference?

A   The supplier sent an invoice for $150 which you have not yet received

B   The supplier has allowed you $150 cash discount which you had omitted to enter in your ledgers

C   You have paid the supplier $150 which he has not yet accounted for

D   You have returned goods worth $150 which the supplier has not yet accounted for

286 The balance on a business's receivables ledger control account was $1,586. It was then discovered that the sales day book for the period had been undercast by $100 and the cash book receipts had been overcast by $100.

What is the correct balance on the receivables ledger control account?

A $1,386

B $1,586

C $1,686

D $1,786

287 The balance on the payables ledger control account was $3,446. It was then discovered that the total from the cash book payments during the period had been posted as $14,576 instead of $14,756. It was also discovered that a contra with the receivables ledger control account of $392 had not been posted at all.

What is the correct balance on the payables ledger control account?

A $2,874

B $3,234

C $3,658

D $4,018

288 Vic's receivables ledger balances add up to $50,000, which does not agree with his receivables control account.

What should the total of the balances on his receivables ledger be after correcting the following errors?

1   A bank credit transfer from a credit customer of $750 was not recorded in the receivables ledger.

2   A contra entry of $2,000 was entered in the control account but not in the receivables and payables ledgers.

A $52,750

B $50,000

C $49,250

D $47,250

289 The following information is available about a business:

Opening payables	$23,450
Closing payables	$25,600
Payments for purchases in the period	$87,350

Of the payments $17,850 represented cash purchases. What is the value of purchases made on credit for the period?

A $85,200

B $67,350

C $89,500

D $71,650

ADJUSTMENTS TO THE TRIAL BALANCE

290 Into which statement of profit or loss columns of the extended trial balance should the balances for sales returns and purchases returns be extended?

	Sales returns	*Purchases returns*
A	Debit	Debit
B	Debit	Credit
C	Credit	Debit
D	Credit	Credit

291 Louise is completing her extended trial balance. In the statement of profit or loss columns, the total of the debit column is greater than the total of the credit column.

Which of the following could explain this?

A   Louise has overstated the credit entry for closing inventory

B   Louise has not made any entries for the post-trial balance adjustments

C   Louise has made a profit

D   Louise has made a loss

292 James has been advised that one of his customers has ceased trading and that it is almost certain that he will not recover the balance of $720 owed by this customer.

What adjustment is required to write off this amount in the extended trial balance?

	Debit	*Credit*
A	Receivables' ledger control account	Irrecoverable debts
	Being write off of irrecoverable amount	
B	Irrecoverable debts	Receivables' ledger control account
	Being write off of irrecoverable amount	
C	Receivables' ledger control account	Bank
	Being write off of irrecoverable amount	
D	Bank	Receivables' ledger control account
	Being write off of irrecoverable amount	

293 At 30 April 20X7 the total amount owed to James by his customers was $54,864. At the same date, James calculated that his receivables allowance is $3,775.

How should these balances be reported in James' statement of financial position?

A $51,089 as a current asset

B $51,089 as a current liability

C $54,864 as a current asset, and $3,775 as a current liability

D $54,864 as a current liability, and $3,775 as a current asset

294 George is preparing the general ledger journal entry to write off an irrecoverable debt. He knows that the debit entry should be made in the receivables expense account.

Into which general ledger account should the credit entry be made?

A Sales account

B Bank account

C Receivables account

D Receivables allowance account

295 Minnie calculated that her receivables allowance at 30 April 20X7 should be $890. At 1 May 20X6, her receivables allowance was $770.

How should the movement in the receivables allowance be recorded in Minnie's statement of profit or loss?

A A charge of $890

B A credit of $890

C A charge of $120

D A credit of $120

296 The revenue generated by Barker Co was $2 million and its accounts receivable were equivalent to 5% of revenue. Following a review of receivables at the year end, Barker Co required an allowance for receivables of $4,000, which would make the allowance one-third higher than the current allowance.

How will Barker Co's profit for the period be affected by the change in allowance?

A Profit will be reduced by $1,000

B Profit will be increased by $1,000

C Profit will be reduced by $1,333

D Profit will be increased by $1,333

297 During the year ended 31 December 20X9 Folland's revenue totalled $3,000,000 and its accounts receivable amounted to 4% of sales revenue for the year. At 31 December 20X9, Folland wishes have an allowance for receivables of $3,600, and discovered that this allowance is 25% higher than it was at 31 December 20X8. During the year ended 31 December 20X9, specific irrecoverable amounts of $3,200 were written off and irrecoverable debts (written off three years previously) of $150 were recovered.

What was the net charge to profit or loss for irrecoverable debts and allowance for receivables for the year ended 31 December 20X9?

A $3,450

B $3,770

C $3,920

D $3,600

298 At the beginning of its accounting period a business had accounts receivable of $13,720 after deducting an allowance for receivables of $630. At the year end, accounts receivable before any allowances amounted to $17,500 and an allowance for receivables of $525 was required.

What is the charge or credit to profit or loss in relation to the change in the allowance for receivables for the year?

A $525 Debit to profit or loss

B $735 Debit to profit or loss

C $105 Credit to profit or loss

D $420 Credit to profit or loss

299 An irrecoverable debt of $1,500 that was written off two years ago was unexpectedly recovered and entered in the trade receivables' ledger column in the cash book.

What accounting entries are required, assuming that the receipt was treated as cash received from a current receivable, to correctly account for this receipt?

	Debit	*Credit*
A	Irrecoverable debts	Trade receivables'' ledger control
B	Receivables' ledger control account	Irrecoverable debts
C	Suspense account	Irrecoverable debts account
D	No adjustment will be necessary	

300 At 30 September 20X4, Z had an allowance for receivables of $37,000.

During the year ended 30 September 20X5 Z wrote off debts totalling $18,000, and at 30 September 20X5 it was decided that the allowance for receivables should be $20,000.

What was included in profit or loss for irrecoverable debts and allowance for receivables?

A $35,000 debit

B $1,000 debit

C $38,000 debit

D $1,000 credit

301 At 30 November 20X6 the balance on Claire's receivables ledger was $37,890. At that date, Clare decided to write off balances totalling $1,570. She also calculated that the allowance for receivables should be increased from $250 to $1,158 at 30 November 20X6.

What was the net receivables balance that was reported in Claire's statement of financial position at 30 November 20X6?

A $35,412

B $35,162

C $36,320

D $36,070

302 **What adjustments are required in the extended trial balance to write off an irrecoverable balance due from a customer?**

A   Debit Revenue, and Credit Receivables expense

B   Debit Irrecoverable debts, and Credit Revenue

C   Debit Irrecoverable debts, and Credit Trade receivables' ledger control

D   Debit Trade receivables' ledger control, and Credit Irrecoverable debts

303 Sybil's financial year ended on 30 November 20X2. The last invoice paid for telephone calls was for $1,800. This invoice covered the three months to 31 October 20X2.

What adjustment is required when preparing the accounts for the year to 30 November 20X2?

A   A prepayment of $600

B   A prepayment of $1,200

C   An accrual of $600

D   An accrual of $1,200

The following information relates to questions 304 to 308.

The following trial balance has been extracted from the books of Tayo as at 30 June 20X2.

	$	$
Administration costs	19,000	
Bank overdraft		800
Cost of sales	166,900	
Non-current assets (cost)	540,000	
Non-current assets (accumulated depreciation)	150,000	
Loan (repayable 20X7)		100,000
Capital account		107,000
Accounts payable ledger control	19,200	
Sales revenue		495,000
Accounts receivable ledger control		37,000
Selling expenses	22,000	
Inventory as at 30 June 20X2	15,100	
Suspense account		192,400
	———	———
	932,200	932,200
	———	———

Following an investigation into the reasons for the large difference in the trial balance totals and discovered the following problems:

(i)   The balance on the suspense account is the difference between the two trial balance columns.

(ii)   Tayo's inexperienced bookkeeper entered some of the account balances in the wrong column of the trial balance.

(iii) The $14,000 balance on bank interest and charges account has been omitted from the trial balance altogether.

(iv) The plant and equipment depreciation charge of $60,000 has been correctly entered in the Accumulated Depreciation account, but no other entry had been made. The depreciation charge is classified as a cost of sale.

(v) The sales day book for June 20X8 was undercast by $5,000.

(vi) A refund of $1,000 for defective stationery was debited to both the bank account and to the administration costs account.

When all errors and omissions have been corrected, the suspense account balance will be cleared and the debit and credit totals of the trial balance will agree.

Note: in the exam, all questions will be independent, and not based on a common scenario.

---

304 **What are the balances that are on the wrong side of the trial balance?**

    A   Bank overdraft, non-current assets (cost), accounts payable control

    B   Cost of sales, loan, accounts receivable control

    C   Non-current assets (accumulated depreciation), sales revenue, share capital

    D   Non-current assets (accumulated depreciation), accounts payable control, accounts receivable control

305 **Which of the following accounting entries would correct the omission of the bank interest and charges account balance?**

	Debit	Credit
A	Bank interest and charges	Bank loan
B	Bank loan	Bank interest and charges
C	Bank interest and charges	Suspense
D	Suspense	Bank interest and charges

306 **Which of the following accounting entries would correct the omission of the plant and equipment depreciation charge?**

	Debit	Credit
A	Cost of sales	Suspense
B	Suspense	Cost of sales
C	Cost of sales	Non-current assets depreciation
D	Non-current assets depreciation	Cost of sales

307 **What accounting entries are required to correct the undercast of the sales day book?**

	Debit	Credit
A	Trade receivables' ledger control	Suspense
B	Suspense	Sales revenue
C	Sales revenue	Trade receivables'' ledger control
D	Trade receivables' ledger control	Sales revenue

308 **What accounting entries are required to correct the error made when accounting for the refund received following the return of defective stationery?**

	Debit	Credit
A	Bank interest and charges	Bank loan
B	Bank loan	Bank interest and charges
C	Bank interest and charges	Suspense
D	Suspense	Bank interest and charges

309 The trial balance of C did not agree, and a suspense account was opened for the difference. Checking the bookkeeping entries for the accounting period revealed a number of errors:

Error

1    $4,600 paid for motor van repairs was correctly treated in the cash book, but was credited to motor vehicles asset account.

2    $360 received from Brown, a credit customer, was credited in error to the account of Green, another credit customer.

3    $9,500 paid for rent was debited to the rent account as $5,900.

4   The total of the discount received column in the cash book had been credited to the revenue account.

5   No entries had been made to record a cash sale of $100.

Which of the errors above would require an entry to the suspense account as part of the process of correcting them?

A   Errors 3 and 4 only

B   Errors 1 and 3 only

C   Errors 2 and 5 only

D   Errors 2 and 3 only

310 The trial balance totals of Gamma at 30 September 20X3 are:

Debit $992,640

Credit $1,026,480

Which two of the following possible errors could, when corrected, cause the trial balance to agree?

Error

1   A payment of $6,160 for insurance has not been entered in the accounts.

2   The balance on the motor expenses account $27,680 has incorrectly been listed in the trial balance as a credit.

3      $6,160 proceeds from the sale of a motor vehicle have been posted to the debit of motor vehicles asset account.

4   The balance of $21,520 on the rent payable account has been omitted from the trial balance.

A   Errors 1 and 2

B   Errors 2 and 3

C   Errors 2 and 4

D   Errors 3 and 4

311 The trial balance of Delta did not agree, and a suspense account was opened for the difference. The following errors were subsequently identified:

Error

1   A cash refund due to customer A was correctly treated in the cash book and then credited to the sales ledger account of customer B.

2   The sale of goods to a director for $300 was recorded by debiting sales revenue account and crediting the director's current account.

3   The depreciation charge for the year had been debited to the irrecoverable debts account The other part of the accounting entry had been made correctly.

4   Some of the cash received from customers had been used to pay sundry expenses before banking the money and had not been recorded.

5      $5,800 paid for plant repairs was correctly treated in the cash book and then credited to plant and equipment asset account.

Which of the above errors would require an entry to the suspense account as part of the process of correcting them?

A   Errors 1, 3 and 5 only

B   Errors 1, 2 and 5 only

C   Errors 1 and 5 only

D   Errors 3 and 4 only

312 A suspense account was opened when a trial balance failed to agree. The following errors were later identified and, when corrected, cleared the suspense account:

Error

1   A gas bill of $420 had been recorded in the Gas account as $240.

2   A stationery purchase of $50 had been entered in the petty cash book and credited to Heat and light account.

3   Interest received of $70 had been entered in the bank account only.

What was the balance on the suspense account before the errors were corrected?

A   Debit $210

B   Credit $210

C   Debit $160

D   Credit $160

313   Which of the following statements about a trial balance is/are correct?

(i)   If the total of the debit balances equals the total of the credit balances, no errors have been made in posting to the general ledger.

(ii)   The trial balance always records non-current assets at market value.

A   (i) only

B   (ii) only

C   Both (i) and (ii)

D   Neither (i) nor (ii)

314 A trial balance has been extracted and a suspense account opened when it failed to balance. One item related to an error of posting an amount of $200, being discounts received from suppliers, to the wrong side of the discounts received account.

What accounting entries are required to correct this error?

	$	Debit	$	Credit
A	200	Discount received	200	Suspense account
B	200	Suspense	200	Discounts received
C	400	Discounts received	400	Suspense
D	400	Suspense	400	Discounts received

315   Which of the following items will not cause an entry to be made in a suspense account?

A   Drawings shown on the credit side of the trial balance

B   Discounts received shown on the credit side of the trial balance

C   Omission of an irrecoverable debt written off from the trial balance

D   The entry of cash in hand ($1,680) on the trial balance as $1,860

316 Jones, a sole trader, has extracted a trial balance and needed to insert a suspense account to make it balance. He has discovered the following errors:

Error

1   Opening inventory of $1,475 has been listed in the trial balance as a credit balance of $1,745.

2   The sales for November ($5,390 inclusive of sales tax) had been correctly entered in the control account and the sales account but no entry had been made in the sales tax account. The amount entered in the sales account was $4,600.

3   The opening accrual for telephone charges of $190 had been brought forward on the wrong side of the telephone expense account.

What was the suspense account balance that Jones included in the trial balance?

A $2,050 Dr

B $2,050 Cr

C $2,840 Dr

D $2,840 Cr

317 An accountant is attempting to resolve a suspense account difference. One of the errors relates to the mis-posting of an amount of $3,079 of sales tax on purchases to the wrong side of the sales tax account.

What will be the correcting entry?

	$	Debit	$	Credit
A	6,158	Sales tax	6,168	Suspense
B	6,158	Suspense	6,158	Sales tax
C	3,079	Sales tax	3,079	Suspense
D	3,079	Suspense	3,079	Sales tax

318 A suspense account shows a credit balance of $130.

What could be the reason for the suspense account balance?

A   Omitting a sale of $130 from the sales ledger

B   Recording a purchase of $130 twice in the purchases account

C   Failing to write off an irrecoverable debt of $130

D   Recording an electricity bill paid of $65 by debiting the bank account and crediting the electricity account

319 The totals of the profit or loss and the statement of financial position columns are:

	Profit or loss		Statement of financial position	
	Dr	Cr	Dr	Cr
	$231,816	$281,917	$136,778	$86,677

Assume that the extended trial balance has been extended, but the profit or loss for the year has not yet been calculated.

What is the profit for the year?

$ [_____]

320 Tina is preparing her accounts for the year to 30 September 20X4 using an extended trial balance. After extending and completing the extended trial balance, the totals are:

	Profit or loss		Statement of financial position	
	Dr	Cr	Dr	Cr
	$	$	$	$
	148,990	136,909	149.608	161,689

What is Tina's loss for the year ended 30 September 20X4?

$ [_____]

321 Priscilla is completing her extended trial balance, which includes balances for depreciation expense and accumulated depreciation.

Into which columns should these balances be extended?

	Depreciation expense	Accumulated depreciation
A	Profit or loss statement debit	Profit or loss statement credit
B	Statement of financial position credit	Statement of financial position debit
C	Profit or loss statement debit	Statement of financial position credit
D	Statement of financial position debit	Profit or loss statement credit

322 When Mervyn's trial balance was extracted, the total of the debit balances was $500 more than the total of the credit balances.

Which of the following errors is a possible explanation for the difference?

A   A cash sale for $250 had not been recorded

B   A cash sale for $250 had been recorded twice

C   A cash sale for $250 had been posted to the credit side of both the sales account and the cash account

D   A cash sale for $250 had been posted to the debit side of both the sales account and the cash account

323 Bert has extracted the following list of balances from his general ledger at 31 October 20X5:

	$
Sales	258,542
Opening inventory	9,649
Purchases	142,958
Expenses	34,835
Non-current assets (NBV)	63,960
Receivables	31,746
Payables	13,864
Cash at bank	1,783
Capital	12,525

What is the total of the debit balances in Bert's trial balance at 31 October 20X5?

A $267,049

B $275,282

C $283,148

D $284,931

324 Two common types of error in bookkeeping are:

- an error of principle
- an error of transposition.

Which of the following correctly states whether or not these errors will be revealed by extracting a trial balance?

	Errors of principle	*Errors of transposition*
A	Will be revealed	Will **not** be revealed
B	Will be revealed	Will be revealed
C	Will **not** be revealed	Will **not** be revealed
D	Will **not** be revealed	Will be revealed

325 Colin bought stationery on credit for $430 but recorded it as $340. When he extracted his trial balance, the total of the debit balances was $157,728.

When the error is corrected, what is the revised total of the debit balances?

A $157,388

B $157,638

C $157,818

D $157,728

326 Which of the following errors should be detected by preparing a trial balance?

    A   A credit entry made on the debit side of the correct account

    B   A credit entry made on the credit side of the wrong account

    C   A transaction for which no entries were made

    D   A transaction entered in the general ledger twice

327 When Jan's trial balance was extracted, the total of the debit balances was $450 less than the total of the credit balances so a suspense account was opened. When she checked, Jan found that:

    (i)   a supplier's invoice for $225 had been debited to both the expense account and the payables control account

    (ii)   a cash sale for $900 had been omitted from the accounting records.

When these errors are corrected, what is the debit balance remaining on the suspense account?

$ _____

328 When carrying out the reconciliation of the balance on the receivables ledger control account with the list of balances from the receivables ledger, Tom found the following:

    (i)   the total of the sales day book was overcast by $90

    (ii)   a sales invoice for T. Blair was posted to J. Blair's account

    (iii)   an invoice to a customer for $650 had been recorded as $560 in the sales day book.

Which of the errors will require an entry in the general ledger?

    A   (i), (ii) and (iii)

    B   (i) and (ii) only

    C   (i) and (iii) only

    D   (ii) and (iii) only

329 Gladys has prepared her draft final accounts, which show a net profit of $24,952 and closing capital of $75,841. She has now found that a supplier's invoice for $250 for advertising expenses was not recorded in her general ledger.

When the error is corrected, what are the revised balances for net profit and capital?

	Net profit	*Capital*
A	$24,702	$75,591
B	$24,702	$76,091
C	$25,202	$75,591
D	$25,202	$76,091

330 Naomi has calculated that her result for the year is a profit.

In which columns of the extended trial balance should Naomi make entries for the profit for the year?

	Profit or loss	*Statement of financial position*
A	Debit	Debit
B	Debit	Credit
C	Credit	Debit
D	Credit	Credit

331 When Nicola extracted her trial balance, the total of the debit balances exceeded the total of the credit balances by $1,000. She opened a suspense account to make the two totals equal. She then discovered that an invoice received for property repairs for $1,500 was entered as $500 on the credit side of the property repairs account.

What is the revised balance on the suspense account after Nicola corrects this error?

A   Nil

B $2,000 debit

C $2,000 credit

D $3,000 credit

332 Chris is completing his extended trial balance. The value of closing inventory had been recorded in the adjustment columns.

Into which columns should the entries for closing inventory be extended?

A   profit or loss statement debit and profit or loss statement credit

B   Statement of financial position debit and statement of financial position credit

C   Profit or loss statement debit and statement of financial position credit

D   Profit or loss statement credit and statement of financial position debit

333 When Paul's extended trial balance was extended and totalled, the totals were:

Statement of profit or loss		*Statement of financial position*	
Debit	*Credit*	*Debit*	*Credit*
$97,945	$120,634	$84,752	$62,063

What is Paul's profit or loss for the year?

A $22,689 loss

B $22,689 profit

C $35,882 loss

D $35,882 profit

334 Cathy is extending the entries for depreciation on her extended trial balance (ETB).

Into which ETB columns should the entries for depreciation charge and accumulated depreciation be extended?

	Depreciation charge	*Accumulated depreciation*
A	Profit or loss statement debit	Statement of financial position debit
B	Profit or loss statement debit	Statement of financial position credit
C	profit or loss statement credit	Statement of financial position credit
D	Profit or loss statement credit	Statement of financial position debit

FINAL ACCOUNTS

335 At 31 October 20X6 Gina Dobbs owed her suppliers $13,856. During the year to 31 October 20X7, her payments to suppliers totalled $95,886, and at 31 October 20X7 she owed $11,552.

What is the value of Gina's credit purchases for the year ended 31 October 20X7?

$ [   ]

336 In the year to 30 November 20X7, Grace Smith obtained a 25% mark up on all her sales. Her sales for the year totalled $120,600. Her opening inventory was valued at $9,340 and her closing inventory was valued at $11,855.

What was the value of Grace's purchases for the year to 30 November 20X7?

$ [   ]

337 Jean's electricity expense account has a debit balance of $1,540. Jean had no opening accrual or prepayment for electricity. The last electricity invoice was for $462 for the three months to 30 September 20X7.

What are the correct amounts to be charged to Jean's statement of profit or loss for the year to 30 November 20X7 and reported as an accrual on her statement of financial position at 30 November 20X7 for electricity?

	Profit or loss charge	*Accrual*
A	$1,694	$154
B	$1,694	$308
C	$1,848	$154
D	$1,848	$308

338   On 1 December 20X6 Pat borrowed $40,000 at a fixed rate of interest. A single capital repayment is due on 1 December 20X9. During the year to 30 November 20X7 the interest of $300 per month was paid on the last day of each month.

How should the loan be reported on Pat's Statement of financial position at 30 November 20X7?

	Current liability	Non-current liability
A	$3,600	$40,000
B	$40,000	$3,600
C	Nil	$40,000
D	$40,000	Nil

The following information relates to questions 339 and 340.

At 31 May 20X8, Janet's general ledger included the following balances:

Trade receivables	$137,850
Receivables allowance at 1 June 20X7	$2,492

Janet has calculated that her receivables allowance should be revised to $2,757.

Note: in the exam, all questions will be independent, and not based on a common scenario.

339   **What amount should be reported in Janet's profit or loss for the change to the allowance for receivables?**

A   a charge of $265

B   a credit of $265

C   a charge of $2,757

D   a credit of $2,757

340   **How should receivables be reported on Janet's statement of financial position at 31 May 20X8?**

A   Current asset of $137,850 and current liability of $2,757

B   Current asset of $135,093

C   Current asset of $137,850 and current liability of $2,492

D   Current asset of $135,358

341   After Toni prepared her draft accounts she discovered that she had incorrectly classified an item of revenue expenditure as capital expenditure.

When the error is corrected, how will Toni's net profit and capital be affected?

	Net profit	Capital
A	Increased	Reduced
B	Reduced	Increased
C	Increased	Increased
D	Reduced	Reduced

342   Which of the following items should be included in the calculation of gross profit?

    A   Carriage inwards

    B   Carriage outwards

    C   Irrecoverable debts written off

    D   Early settlement discount received

343   How should each of the following items be classified in the financial statements?

	Current asset	Non-current asset
Assets which will be converted into cash as part of normal business activity		
Assets which are used to increase productive capacity of the business		

344   On 1 November 20X4 Leah took out a business development loan of $30,000. The loan is to be repaid in ten equal six-monthly instalments. Leah made the first repayment of $3,000 on 1 May 20X5.

    How should the outstanding balance of $27,000 be reported on Leah's statement of financial position at 31 May 20X5?

	Current liability	Non-current liability
A	Nil	$27,000
B	$6,000	$21,000
C	$21,000	$6,000
D	$27,000	Nil

345   Darren is a second-hand car dealer. If a car develops a fault within 30 days of the sale, Darren will repair it free of charge. At 30 April 20X4 Darren had made a provision for repairs of $2,500. At 30 April 20X5 he calculated that his provision should be $2,000.

    What entry should be made for the provision in Darren's statement of profit or loss for the year to 30 April 20X5?

    A   A charge of $500

    B   A credit of $500

    C   A charge of $2,000

    D   A credit of $2,000

346   What is the main purpose of a statement of financial position?

    A   To report the current value of the business

    B   To indicate if the business is trading profitably

    C   To report the assets and liabilities of the business

    D   To report the personal assets of the business owner

347 William's trial balance at 30 September 20X5 included the following balances:

Trade receivables $75,943

Receivables allowance $4,751

How should these balances be reported in William's statement of financial position as at 30 September 20X5?

A   An asset of $71,192

B   An asset of $75,943 and a liability of $4,751

C   A liability of $71,192

D   A liability of $75,943 and an asset of $4,751

348 Harvey's trial balance included a balance for his drawings.

How should this balance be treated in the final accounts?

A   As an expense in the statement of profit or loss

B   As income in the statement of profit or loss

C   As a reduction in capital

D   As an increase in capital

349 **What entries should be made in a sole trader's capital account to record a loss for the year and drawings?**

	Loss	Drawings
A	Debit	Debit
B	Credit	Credit
C	Debit	Debit
D	Debit	Credit

350 Heather is completing her extended trial balance.

Into which columns should Heather extend the balances for closing inventory?

	Statement of profit or loss	Statement of financial position
A	Debit	Credit
B	Credit	Debit
C	Debit	Debit
D	Credit	Credit

351 At 31 May 20X7 Katie had a loan with an outstanding balance of $30,000. She is required to repay $500 on the 10th day of each month.

How should the loan be reported on her statement of financial position at 31 May 20X7?

A   As a current liability of $30,000

B   As a current liability of $24,000 and a non-current liability of $6,000

C   As a current liability of $6,000 and a non-current liability of $24,000

D   As a non-current liability of $30,000

352 Pat does not keep a full set of accounting records, but the following information is available for the month of June 20X9:

	$
Accounts receivable, 1 June 20X9	800
Accounts receivable, 30 June 20X9	550
Credit sales	6,800
Cash received from customers (credit)	6,730
Irrecoverable written off	40
Allowance for receivables established 30 June 20X9	100

Assuming that there were no other transactions, what was the value of contras between the receivables' ledger control account and the payables' ledger control account during the month?

$ [   ]

The following information relates to questions 353 to 357.

Carol has been in business as a freelance graphics designer for several years. She does not use the double-entry system to maintain detailed bookkeeping records. Instead, she analyses cash receipts and payments on a spreadsheet. She also keeps track of the amounts due from customers and owing to payables by means of a simple computerised record.

Carol's opening statement of financial position, as at 31 December 20X8, was as follows:

	Cost	Aggregate depreciation	Carrying value
	$	$	$
Furniture	800	200	600
Computer	2,800	1,225	1,575
Printer	1,500	656	844
	5,100	2,081	3,019

Current assets

Inventory of stationery and printer consumables	550
Accounts receivable	800
Bank	700
	2,050

Current liabilities

Accounts payable	70
	1,980
	4,999

Long-term liabilities

Bank loan	2,400
	2,599
Capital	2,599

Carol's analysis of cash receipts and payments for the year ended 31 December 20X9 was as follows:

	Receipts $		Payments $
Received from clients	28,000	Drawings	24,000
Additional loan	2,000	Bank interest	400
		Suppliers of stationery and printer consumables	1,800
		Sundry expenses	600
	30,000		26,800

Carol's closing inventory of stationery cost $900. Her accounts receivable totalled $1,300 and she owed $200 to her suppliers. Furniture should be depreciated at 25% straight line and the computer and printer at 25% reducing balance.

Note: in the exam, all questions will be independent, and not based on a common scenario.

353 What was the value of Carol's sales figure for the year?

- A $27,500
- B $29,300
- C $28,500
- D $26,700

354 What was the cost of Carol's purchases figure for the year?

- A $1,930
- B $1,670
- C $2,000
- D $1,600

355 **What was Carol's depreciation charge for the year?**

A $755

B $805

C $1,225

D $1,275

356 **What was Carol's capital at the year end?**

A $3,714

B $4,400

C $8,114

D $8,314

357 **What was Carol's profit for the year?**

A $23,865

B $25,115

C $25,801

D $29,515

358 A business purchased goods on credit for $10,000; half the goods purchased were sold for cash at a mark-up of 120%. Sales commission of 5% was payable on this transaction. All takings were banked.

What was the net profit arising as a result of entering into these transactions?

$

359 The following information is relevant to the calculation of the sales figure for Alpha, a sole trader who does not keep proper accounting records:

	$
Opening accounts receivable	29,100
Cash received from credit customers and paid into the bank	381,600
Expenses paid out of cash received from credit customers before banking	6,800
Irrecoverable debts written off	7,200
Refunds to credit customers	2,100
Contra with payables ledger control	9,400
Cash sales	112,900
Closing accounts receivable	38,600

What figure should be included in Alpha's trading account for sales revenue?

A $525,300

B $511,700

C $529,500

D $510,900

360 Paolo is a sole proprietor whose accounting records are incomplete. All the sales are cash sales and during the month $50,000 was banked, including $5,000 from the sale of a business car. He paid $12,000 wages in cash from the till and withdrew $2,000 per month as drawings. The cash in the till at the beginning and end of the month was $300 and $400 respectively. There were no other payments during the month.

What were the sales for the month?

A $58,900

B $59,100

C $63,900

D $64,100

361 At 31 December 20X2, FCA Co had $100 in the cash till and it was discovered that some cash had been stolen.

At 1 January 20X2, there was $50 in the cash till and receivables were $2,000. Total sales for 20X2 were $230,000. Accounts receivable at 31 December 20X2 were $3,000. During 20X2, cheques banked from credit sales were $160,000 and cash sales of $50,000 have been banked.

How much cash was stolen during 20X2?

$

362 A business operates on a gross profit margin of 33⅓%. Gross profit on a sale was $800, and expenses were $680.

What is the net profit percentage?

A   20%

B   15%

C   10%

D   5%

363 At 1 November 20X4 Brian owed $28,754 to his suppliers. During the year he paid his suppliers a total of $185,844. At 31 October 20X5 he owed $26,189.

What was the value of Brian's credit purchases in the year to 31 October 20X5?

$

364 During the year to 30 November 20X5 Amanda bought goods for resale at a cost of $75,550. Her inventory at 1 December 20X4 was valued at $15,740. She did not count her inventory at 30 November 20X5, but she knows that her sales for the year ended 30 November 20X5 were $91,800. All sales were made at a mark-up of 20%.

Based on the information above, what was the value of Amanda's inventory at 30 November 20X5?

$

365 During the year ended 30 April 20X6 Peter's sales were $182,000. All of his sales were made at a mark-up of 30%. His opening inventory value was $11,800 and his closing inventory value was $9,700.

What was the cost of Peter's purchases in the year ended 30 April 20X6?

$ *137900*

366 During June 20X8 Laura bought goods for $12,000. She paid $11,000 of this by cheque immediately and agreed a 30 day credit period for the balance. She intends to buy more goods at a cost of $13,000 in July 20X8.

What liability should be reported for Laura's payables at 30 June 20X8?

$

367 During the year ended 30 April 20X8 Tanya paid a total of $127,569 to her suppliers. Her opening and closing balances due to suppliers and her opening and closing inventory values were:

	Opening value	Closing value
Suppliers	$11,564	$12,826
Inventory	$5,288	$4,184

What was Tanya's cost of sales for the year ended 30 April 20X8?

$

368 For the year ended 31 May 20X8 Lesley's sales totalled $600,000 and her cost of sales totalled $480,000.

What are the correct figures for Lesley's mark up and margin for the year ended 31 May 20X8?

	Mark up	Margin
A	25%	25%
B	25%	20%
C	20%	25%
D	20%	20%

369 For the year ended 31 August 20X2 Anne's sales totalled $850,000 and her cost of sales totalled $680,000.

What are the correct figures for Anne's mark up and margin for the year ended 31 August 20X2?

	Mark up	Margin
A	25%	25%
B	25%	20%
C	20%	25%
D	20%	20%

370 Whilst finalising her financial accounts for the year ended 28 February 20X6, Beryl noticed that she had not yet accounted for a contra between the trade receivables and trade payables ledger control accounts which had been agreed with one of her customers who also supplied goods to her business. The agreed amount of the contra was $2,500.

What are the accounting entries required to account for this contra?

A   Debit discount received, and Credit trade receivables control account

B   Debit trade payables control account, and Credit discount received

C   Debit trade receivables control account, and Credit trade payables control account

D   Debit trade payables control account, and Credit trade receivables control account

371 For the year ended 31 July 20X3 Fred's cost of sales totalled $250,000 and his gross profit totalled $50,000.

What are the correct figures for Fred's mark up and margin for the year ended 31 July 20X3?

	Mark up	Margin
A	20%	16.7%
B	25%	20%
C	16.7%	20%
D	20%	20%

372 At 31 October 20X7 Doreen owed her suppliers $24,786. During the year to 31 October 20X8, her payments to suppliers totalled $104,886 and she received prompt payment discounts of $750. She had also needed to account for a contra between the trade receivables and trade payables control accounts amounting to $500. At 31 October 20X8 she owed $23,552.

What was the cost of Doreen's credit purchases for the year ended 31 October 20X8?

$

373 In the year ended 30 November 20X5, Lydia earned a 20% mark-up on cost on all sales made. Her sales for the year totalled $240,600. Her opening inventory was valued at $13,340 and her closing inventory was valued at $17,855.

What was the cost of Lydia's purchases for the year ended 30 November 20X5?

A $192,480

B $195,985

C $200,500

D $205,015

374 At 1 July 20X4 Alison was owed $30,468 by her customers. During the year to 30 June 20X5, her receipts from credit customers amounted to $105,382 and she had irrecoverable debts amounting to 2,500. She also needed to account for a contra between trade receivables' and trade payables' control accounts amounting to $1,000. At 30 June 20X5 she was owed $27,532.

What was the value of Alison's credit sales for the year ended 30 June 20X5?

$ [   ]

375 At 1 April 20X3 Nick was owed $22,785 by his customers. During the year to 31 March 20X4, his receipts from credit customers amounted to $95,723 and he agreed contras with credit customers who were also supplied him with goods on credit of $3,750. Nick also wrote off an irrecoverable receivable of $350 during the year. At 31 March 20X4 he was owed $24,680 by his credit customers.

What was the value of Nick's credit sales for the year ended 31 March 20X4?

A $101,718

B $97,968

C $97,618

D $101,368

376 At 1 July 20X7 David was owed $32,785 by his customers. During the year to 30 June 20X8, his receipts from credit customers amounted to $87,654. He agreed contras with other credit customers who were also suppliers to his business of $2,193 and received discounts of £3,219. David wrote off an irrecoverable receivable of $127 during the year. In August 20X7, $250 was received in respect of a receivable which had been written off in the previous accounting year which is not included within the total received from credit customers. At 31 March 20X4 he was owed $30,123 by his credit customers.

What was the value of Dave's credit sales for the year ended 30 June 20X8?

A $84,220

B $87,312

C $87,562

D $87,062

377 Luigi is a sole proprietor whose accounting records are incomplete. All the sales are cash sales and during the September 20X4 $34,200 was banked, including $3,250 from the sale of an old machine.

Also during September 20X4, Luigi paid $3,500 wages in cash from the till and withdrew $1,500 as drawings. The cash in the till at 1 September 20X4 and at 30 September 20X4 was $250 and $350 respectively. There were no other payments during September 20X4.

What was the value of sales made in September 20X4?

A $36,450

B $39,300

C $36,050

D $36,120

378 Fernando is a sole proprietor whose accounting records are incomplete. All the sales are cash sales and during May 20X1 $87,654 was banked, including $10,000 capital introduced.

During May 20X1, Fernando paid $8,750 wages in cash from the till and withdrew $1,825 as drawings. During May 20X1, Fernando also purchased a new laptop for business use, paying $750 cash. The cash in the till at 31 May 20X1 was $50 and at 1 May 20X1 was $70. There were no other payments during May 20X1.

What was the value of sales made in May 20X1?

A $88,979

B $88,209

C $98,959

D $88,959

379 Alvaro is a sole proprietor whose accounting records are incomplete. All the sales are cash sales and during August 20X5 $67,890 was banked.

During August 20X5, Alvaro withdrew $500 as drawing and paid $6,750 wages in cash from the till. The cash in the till at 1 August 20X5 was $100 and there was $200 in the cash till at 31 August 20X5. During August 20X5, Alvaro paid a repair bill of £350 in cash and paid for some purchases in cash, amounting to $3,728. In addition, he made a cash refund to a customer of $100 for return of goods. There were no other payments during August 20X5.

What was the value of sales made for the month of August 20X5?

A $79,318

B $79,418

C $79,068

D $79,518

380 Wilma's trial balance at 30 November 20X2 included the following balances:

Machinery – at cost $85,493

Machinery – accumulated depreciation $7,514

How should these balances be reported in Wilma's statement of financial position as at 30 November 20X2?

A   A liability of $77,979

B   An asset of $85,493 and a liability of $7,514

C   An asset of $77,979

D   A liability of $85,493 and an asset of $7,514

381 Hillary's trial balance included an account balance for drawings made during the year.

How should this balance be treated in Hillary's final accounts?

A   As an expense in the statement of profit or loss

B   As income in the statement of profit or loss

C   As a reduction in capital

D   As an increase in capital

382 Jurgen is a sole proprietor whose accounting records are incomplete. All sales are made for cash and during November 20X7 $26,543 was banked.

During November 20X7, Jurgen withdrew $1750 for personal use and paid $3,750 wages in cash from the till. Jurgen also purchased new office furniture and equipment, paying $1,750 cash. The cash in the till at 30 November 20X7 was $50 and $70 at 1 November 20X7. There were no other payments made during November 20X7.

What was the value of Jurgen's cash sales for November 20X7?

$\boxed{\text{\$} \qquad\qquad}$

383 For the year ended 30 September 20X5 Emre's sales were $825,000. All of his sales were made at a mark-up of 25%. His opening inventory value was $12,800 and his closing inventory value was $14,700.

What was the cost of Emre's purchases for the year ended 30 September 20X5?

$\boxed{\text{\$} \qquad\qquad}$

384 At 1 April 20X5 Carole owed her suppliers $21,876. During the year ended 31 March 20X6, her payments to suppliers totalled $123,456 and she received prompt payment discounts of $1,025. She also needed to account for a contra between the trade receivables and trade payables control accounts amounting to $2,500. At 31 October 20X8 she owed $19,998.

What was the cost of Carole's credit purchases for the year ended 31 March 20X6?

$\boxed{\text{\$} \qquad\qquad}$

PARTNERSHIPS

385 **Which of the following statements provides the definition of a partnership?**

A   A maximum of three people in business together

B   Persons in business together with the intention of sharing profits and losses

C   Two work colleagues who are employed by the same business

D   Two persons who each have their own business as a sole proprietor

386 **What is the purpose of a partnership agreement?**

A   It is a legal requirement for all partnerships to have a partnership agreement.

B   It enables customers to understand how the partnership operates.

C   It is a contract between the partners that sets out their rights and responsibilities to each other.

D   It is a contract between the partners that sets out the profit and loss sharing arrangements between the partners.

387 Which of the following items would not normally be included within a partnership agreement?

A   The names of the partners

B   The arrangements for sharing residual profits and losses between the partners

C   The name and business location of the partnership

D   The names of the principal customers and suppliers of the business

---

The following information relates to questions 388 and 389.

Vivienne and Robert are in partnership, sharing profits and losses in a ratio of 3:2. The business maintains current accounts and fixed capital accounts for the partners. In the last year, the profit before appropriations was $27,800. Robert is entitled to an annual salary of $3,800.

During the year Vivienne and Robert made cash drawings of $12,000 each.

Note: in the exam, all questions will be independent, and not based on a common scenario.

---

388 What is Vivienne's share of the profit?

A $2,280

B $9,600

C $14,400

D $16,680

389 The correct entry for the partners' drawings has been made in the cash account.

What entry is needed to complete the posting for the partners' drawings?

A   A debit entry in the partners' capital accounts

B   A credit entry in the partners' capital accounts

C   A debit entry in the partners' current accounts

D   A credit entry in the partners' current accounts

390 Albert and David are in partnership, sharing profits and losses in the ratio 3:2. Under the terms of the partnership agreement, David is entitled to a salary of $8,000. The partnership statement of profit or loss for the year to 30 November 20X4 reported a profit of $16,000.

What is Albert's share of the profit?

$ [   ]

391 Alex and Kim are in partnership. In the year to 31 October 20X6, Alex's drawings were $18,000 and the following entries have been made in the partnership appropriation account for Alex:

	$
Salary	6,500
Interest on drawings	1,800
Share of profit	12,750

At 1 November 20X5, the balance on Alex's current account was $24,800 (credit).

What was the balance on Alex's current account at 31 October 20X6?

$ [   ]

The following information relates to questions 392 to 394.

Hub Design has three partners: Mary, Jenny and Agnes. The three share profits equally after interest on capital at 5% and Jenny's partnership salary of $8,000. The partners' account balances are shown below:

	Mary	Jenny	Agnes	Total
Capital	$20,000	$15,000	$40,000	$75,000
Current	$100,000	$80,000	$110,000	$290,000
Drawings	$30,000	$35,000	$40,000	$105,000

No interest is paid on current account balances.

The net profit for the year ended 31 December 20X6 is $170,000.

Note: in the exam, all questions will be independent, and not based on a common scenario.

---

392 **What will the statement of financial position as at 31 December 20X6 show as the total for owners' equity?**

$ [   ]

393 **What will each partner receive as a share of residual profit?**

$ [   ]

394 **What total profit will Jenny receive for the year ended 31 December 20X6?**

$ [   ]

395 Ingrid and Sam are in partnership sharing profits and losses in the ratio 3:4. The statement of profit or loss for the year to 31 May 20X6 reported a net profit of $30,709. Ingrid is entitled to a salary of $14,000 per annum.

What was Sam's share of the profit for the year to 31 May 20X6?

$ [   ]

396 Hilda and Stan are in partnership sharing profits and losses in the ratio 2:3. The statement of profit or loss for the year ended 31 August 20X3 reported a net profit of $73,540. Hilda is entitled to a salary of $18,000 per annum.

What was Hilda's total share of the profit for the year to 31 August 20X3?

A $40,216

B $22,216

C $33,324

D $51,324

397 Wilma and Jane are in partnership sharing profits and losses in the ratio 6:4. The statement of profit or loss for the year ended 31 January 20X8 reported a net profit of $24,680. Jane is entitled to a salary of $5,000 per annum.

What was Jane's total share of the profit for the year to 31 January 20X8?

A $11,808

B $12,872

C $7,872

D $9,872

398 Paul and Linda are in partnership sharing profits and losses in the ratio 7:3. The statement of profit or loss for the year ended 31 July 20X7 reported a net profit of $52,900. Paul is entitled to an annual salary of $14,000 and Linda is entitled to an annual salary of $6,000.

What was Linda's total share of the profit for the year ended 31 July 20X7?

$

399 Sarah and Geoff are in partnership sharing profits and losses in the ratio 90:10. The statement of profit or loss for the year ended 28 February 20X4 reported a net profit of $36,600. Geoff is entitled to an annual salary of $12,500.

What is Geoff's total share of the profit for the year to 28 February 20X4?

A $3,660

B $34,190

C $21,690

D $14,910

400 Tommy and Angela are in partnership sharing profits and losses in the ratio 3:5. Tommy is also entitled to a salary of $5,000. At 1 June 20X5, the business had the following credit balances on the capital and current accounts of the partners:

	Tommy	Angela
Capital	$80,000	$60,000
Current	$21,735	$14,876

During the year ended 30 June 20X6, Tommy and Angela made drawings of $27,500 and $26,500 respectively. For the year ended 31 May 20X6, the statement of profit or loss for the partnership disclosed a profit of $60,000.

What is the balance on Angela's current account at 31 May 20X6?

A $19,860

B $22,751

C $7,875

D $25,876

401 Kieran and Alison are in partnership sharing profits and losses in the ratio 2:3. Kieran is entitled to a salary of $3,500 and Alison is entitled to a salary of $2,500. At 1 September 20X6, the business had the following credit balances on the partners' capital and current accounts:

	Kieran	Alison
Capital	$80,000	$60,000
Current	$14,769	$13,748

During the year ended 31 August 20X7, Kieran and Alison made drawings of $38,775 and $43,915 respectively. For the year ended 31 August 20X7, the statement of profit or loss for the partnership disclosed a profit of $80,000.

What was the balance on Kieran's current account at 31 August 20X7?

$ _____

The following information relates to questions 402 to 406.

Three's A Crowd has three partners: Alan, Andy and Roger. The three partners share profits equally after interest on capital at 5% and Andy's partnership salary of $12,500. The partners' account balances at 31 July 20X4 are shown below:

	Alan	Andy	Roger
Capital	$20,000	$20,000	$10,000
Current	$7,000	$5,250	$8,375
Drawings	$13,750	$11,250	$9,500

No interest is paid on current account balances.

The net profit for the year ended 31 July 20X4 was $150,000.

Note: in the exam, all questions will be independent, and not based on a common scenario.

402 **What will the statement of financial position as at 31 July 20X4 show as the total for owners' equity?**

    A $186,125

    B $255,125

    C $36,125

    D $165,500

403 **What will each partner receive as a share of residual profit?**

    A $50,000

    B $45,000

    C $49,167

    D $45,833

404 **What total profit will Andy receive for the year ended 31 July 20X4?**

    A $46,000

    B $57,500

    C $58,500

    D $60,000

405 **What will Alan's current account balance be after accounting for the profit share for the year ended 31 July 20X4?**

    A $53,000

    B $38,250

    C $32,250

    D $39,250

406 **What will the total of the partners' current account balances at 31 July 20X4?**

    A $136,125

    B $170,625

    C $205,125

    D $115,500

The following information relates to questions 407 and 408.

'Three's Two Much' has three partners: Ron, Kevin and Sid. The three partners share profits and losses equally after interest on capital at 10% and partnership salaries of $8,000 for Ron, $10,000 for Kevin and $12,000 for Sid. The partners' account balances at 31 July 20X4 are shown below:

	Ron	Kevin	Sid
Capital	$50,000	$50,000	$20,000
Current	$7,000	$5,250	$8,375
Drawings	$13,750	$11,250	$9,500

No interest is paid on current account balances.

The net profit for the year ended 31 July 20X4 was $45,000.

Note: in the exam, all questions will be independent, and not based on a common scenario.

---

407 **What will each partner receive as a share of residual profit or loss for the year?**

    A $1,000 profit

    B $15,000 profit

    C $1,000 loss

    D $5,000 profit

408 **What total profit share will Ron receive for the year ended 31 July 20X4?**

    A $7,000

    B $12,000

    C $13,000

    D $14,000

409 **How should each of the following be accounted for?**

	Business expense	Profit appropriation
Salary paid to an employee		
Salary paid to a partner		

410 Which of the following items would normally be accounted for in the capital account of a partner?

A   Cash introduced upon joining a partnership

B   Cash drawings from the business for personal use

C   Their share of profit or loss for the year

D   Goods withdrawn from the business for personal use

411 Which of the following items would not be accounted for in the current account of a partner?

A   The share of residual profit or loss for the year that the partner is entitled to

B   Accounting for goodwill upon retirement of a partner

C   Interest on capital

D   Interest charged on overdrawn current account balances

The following information relates to questions 412 to 414.

Triple Stripe has three partners: Xavier, Yasmin and Zac. The three partners share profits in the ratio 40:40:20 after interest on capital accounts at 4% and Yasmin's partnership salary of $7,500. The partners' account balances are shown below:

	Xavier	Yasmin	Zak	Total
Capital account at 1 August 20X2	$32,000	$28,000	$20,000	$80,000
Current account at 1 August 20X2	$51,000	$45,000	$25,000	$121,000
Drawings for the year ended 31 July 20X3	$27,000	$32,000	$12,000	$71,000

No interest is paid on current account balances or charged on overdrawn current account balances. The net profit for the year ended 31 July 20X3 was $180,000.

Note: in the exam, all questions will be independent, and not based on a common scenario.

---

412 What was the total for owners' equity in the statement of financial position as at 31 July 20X3?

A $80,000

B $121,000

C $131,000

D $310,000

413 What did Xavier receive as a share of residual profit for the year ended 31 July 20X3?

A $33,860

B $67,720

C $69,000

D $72,000

414 **What total profit share did Yasmin receive for the year ended 31 July 20X3?**

A $72,000

B $67,720

C $76,340

D $75,220

415 Gordon and Delia are in partnership and share profits and losses equally. On 1 January 20X8, Mary is admitted to the partnership and it was agreed that, from that date, profits and losses would be shared equally between the three partners. Goodwill was valued at $60,000. Gordon and Delia had the following credit balances on their capital and current accounts at 1 January 20X8:

	Gordon	Delia
Capital	$60,000	$60,000
Current	$15,000	$10,000

A goodwill account is not maintained in the books of the partnership.

How much is Mary required to contribute if she is to have a capital account credit balance of $10,000 immediately after joining the partnership?

A $10,000

B $20,000

C $30,000

D $60,000

416 Alan, Gary and Mark are in partnership and share profits and losses equally. Alan decided to retire with effect from 31 December 20X7 and it was agreed that he would withdraw cash for the full amount due to him on his capital and current account balances at that date. Goodwill was valued at $60,000 at 31 December 20X7. Gary and Mark will continue in partnership and will share profits and losses in the ratio 30:20 Alan, Gary and Mark had the following credit balances on their capital and current accounts at 31 December 20X7 prior to accounting for Alan's retirement:

	Alan	Gary	Mark
Capital	$60,000	$60,000	40,000
Current	$15,000	$10,000	5,000

A goodwill account is not maintained in the books of the partnership.

How much will Alan withdraw from the partnership at the date of his retirement?

A $55,000

B $95,000

C $65,000

D $25,000

417 John and Terry are in partnership and share profits and losses in the proportion 4:2. On 1 January 20X8, Eric is admitted to the partnership and it was agreed that, from that date, profits and losses would be shared equally between the three partners. Goodwill was valued at $75,000. John and terry had the following credit balances on their capital and current accounts at 1 January 20X8:

	John	Terry
Capital	$50,000	$50,000
Current	$8,000	$7,000

A goodwill account is not maintained in the books of the partnership.

How much is Eric required to contribute if he is to have a capital account credit balance of $5,000 immediately after joining the partnership?

A $10,000

B $20,000

C $30,000

D $60,000

418 Victoria, Emma and Louise are in partnership and share profits and losses equally. Victoria decided to retire with effect from 31 December 20X6 and it was agreed that she would withdraw cash for the full amount due to her on her capital and current account balances at that date. Goodwill was valued at $90,000 at 31 December 20X6. Emma and Louise will continue in partnership and will share profits and losses in the ratio 5:3. Victoria, Emma and Louise had the following credit balances on their capital and current accounts at 31 December 20X6 immediately prior to accounting for Victoria's retirement:

	Victoria	Emma	Louise
Capital	$25,000	$25,000	35,000
Current	$5,000	$10,000	2,000

A goodwill account is not maintained in the books of the partnership.

How much will Victoria withdraw from the partnership at the date of her retirement?

A $55,000

B $30,000

C $55,000

D $60,000

419 **When accounting for goodwill upon admission of a partner, what accounting entries are required to recognise goodwill due to the old partnership?**

	Debit	Credit
A	Goodwill	Partners' capital accounts
B	Goodwill	Partners' current account
C	Partners' capital accounts	Goodwill
D	Partners' current accounts	Goodwill

420 When accounting for goodwill upon admission of a partner, and having accounted for goodwill as an asset, what accounting entries are then required to remove goodwill from the partnership accounting records?

	Debit	Credit
Partners' capital accounts		
Goodwill		

Section 3

ANSWERS TO REVISION QUESTIONS

ACCOUNTING PRINCIPLES AND CONCEPTS

1   Accounting standards improve financial accounting by providing the basis for generally accepted accounting practice (GAAP). This arises because standards:

- reduce variations in accounting practice by specifying how particular issues should be treated

- provide a reference point when choosing between alternative treatments

- encourage debate, which (generally) leads to a commonly accepted practice

- whilst providing a framework, allow a degree of flexibility which may be difficult to achieve through legislation.

2   The going concern concept states that, unless there is evidence to the contrary, accounts should be prepared on the assumption that the business will continue for the foreseeable future, and that it will not be liquidated or significantly reduced in scale. This means that the assets will not be valued at their 'break-up' (individual market) value.

3   **Relevance**

Information is relevant if:

- it will influence the economic decisions of users; and

- it is provided on a timely basis.

Faithful Representation

If information is to represent faithfully the transactions and other events that it purports to represent, they must be accounted for and presented in accordance with their substance and economic reality and not merely their legal form.

To be a perfectly faithful representation, financial information would possess the following characteristics:

(a)   it is complete

(b)   it is free from deliberate or systematic bias (i.e. it is neutral)

(c)   it is free from material error

Enhancing characteristics:

Comparability

This means that information can be compared either with previous periods for the same business or with other businesses.

This is usually achieved by the consistent application of accounting policies from one period to the next, and by disclosure of those policies.

Verifiability

Verifiability is a quality of information that means the information is supportable, i.e. it can be verified.

Verification can be direct or indirect. Direct verification means verifying an amount or other representation through direct observation i.e. counting cash. Indirect verification means checking the inputs to a model, formula or other technique and recalculating the outputs using the same methodology i.e. recalculating inventory amounts using the same cost flow assumption such as first in, first out method.

Timeliness

Timeliness means having information available to decision makers in time to be capable of influencing their decisions. Generally, the older the information is the less useful it becomes.

Understandability

This term means that financial information should be capable of being understood. It should be noted that this test is applied in the context of the users having a reasonable knowledge of accounting and business.

Effectively this means that the formats and disclosures laid down by the regulatory framework should be considered to be minimum requirements, and additional information should be provided as necessary.

4   The business entity concept states that, no matter what the legal status of the business, in accounting terms we always keep the business and the owner separate.

This means that, when recording transactions, we are only concerned with how the business is affected. For example, if the owner introduces capital, we are not concerned with the source of the capital and, apart from increasing the owner's capital balance, we do not record how the owner is affected by the transaction.

5   Transactions are recorded by both a debit entry and a credit entry (also referred to as 'double entry') as this reflects the effects of the transaction on the entity. Every transaction affects the entity in two ways. This is usually referred to as the 'dual aspect'. The two effects mean that the accounting equation (Assets − Liabilities = Capital) will apply consistently to the entity.

For example, if expenses are paid in cash, the entity is affected by an increase in the expense and a reduction in cash. The increase in the expense will cause a reduction in profit, and therefore capital. Thus both assets and capital have reduced, and the accounting equation will continue to apply.

BASIC BOOKKEEPING

6   In the IASB's *Framework for the preparation and presentation of financial statements*, an asset is defined as the right of an entity to access future economic benefits, while a liability is defined as an obligation to transfer future economic benefits to a third party.

In both cases, the right or obligation must have arisen as a result of a past event or transaction.

An example of an asset is an amount owed by customers for goods which have purchased on credit.

The balance due for repayment on a loan is an example of a liability.

7   When goods are purchased on credit, both assets and liabilities will increase by the same amount, but capital will be unaffected. This is because:

- the cost of the items purchased will be included in the inventory of the business

- the liability to suppliers will rise by the same amount; and

- as no profit has been earned, and no expense has been incurred, capital will remain unchanged.

8   When a credit customer is not expected to take advantage of early settlement discount offered, the settlement discount is not deducted in arriving at the invoice price. If the customer, as expected, does not pay early, the amount subsequently paid should match the invoice and receivable previously recorded.

If, however, the customer does pay within the time period to be eligible for the settlement discount, both revenue and the receivable is reduced to match with the cash received. The sales ledger account of the individual customer should also be updated.

9   When a credit customer is expected to take advantage of early settlement discount offered, the settlement discount is deducted in arriving at the invoice price. In this situation, settlement discount is treated in exactly the same way as trade discount and excluded from the invoice price. If the customer, as expected, does pay early, the amount subsequently paid should match the invoice and receivable previously recorded.

If, however, the customer pays outwith time period to be eligible for the settlement discount, the full amount is receivable and the amount received in excess of the revenue and receivable previously recorded is accounted for as additional revenue.

NON-CURRENT ASSETS AND DEPRECIATION

10 There are a number of reasons for a difference between the assets in the non-current asset register and those physically present in the business. For example, the non-current asset register may not have been updated to reflect the purchase of a new asset or the disposal of an old asset. In addition, an error may have been made when an entry was originally made in the records.

11 The factors to consider would be the original cost less depreciation to date, compared with the proceeds from the sale.

12

	Depreciation charge	Cost/Net book value
	$	$
Original cost		15,000
Year 1	15,000 × 25% = 3,750	15,000 – 3,750 = 11,250
year 2	11,250 × 25% = 2,813	11,250 – 2,813 = 8,437
year 3	8,437 × 25% = 2,109	8,437 – 2,109 = 6,328
Year 4	6,328 × 25% = 1,582	6,328 – 1,582 = 4,746
Year 5	4,746 × 25% = 1,187	4,746 – 1,187 = 3,559

CONTROL ACCOUNTS, RECONCILIATIONS AND ERRORS

13 This is an error of principle – an asset, which is a capital expenditure, has been charged to revenue expenditure account. The chairs will be used for a long period of time and should be capitalised and depreciated over their useful economic life.

14 The reasons for disagreement between the cash book and bank statement balances can be: timing differences for unpresented cheques and outstanding lodgements, together with standing order and BACS receipts and payments, and bank charges and interest.

15 Control accounts are maintained for the following reasons:

(1) *Check on accuracy*

By comparing the balance on the control account with the total of the balances on the individual accounts, errors can be highlighted.

(2) *Locating errors*

If an error is made, it will be easier to locate if a regular reconciliation is carried out as there will be fewer transactions to be checked than would be the case if such a reconciliation were not carried out.

(3) *Assist in preparation of final accounts*

As the control account provides a total figure, there is no need to collate the individual balances. This means that the preparation of the final accounts is speeded up.

ADJUSTMENTS TO THE TRIAL BALANCE

16   The main purpose of a trial balance is to ensure that debit balances and credit balances are equal. This provides a basic check on the accuracy of the postings.

17   An irrecoverable debt a debt which is considered to be bad and unlikely to be paid by the customer. Irrecoverable debts are written off as an expense in the statement of profit or loss. The relevant receivables account is reduced accordingly.

An allowance for receivables is made for debts where there is some basis for uncertainty that they will be fully recovered. The business makes an allowance for receivables, based upon objective evidence available. Examples of evidence that may support the creation of an allowance for receivables include: amount due disputed by the customer or goods identified as faulty or not received or the amount is overdue for payment. Any increase or decrease in the allowance is credited or debited to the statement of profit or loss. The full amount of the allowance is deducted from the figure of receivables shown in the statement of financial position. The accounts of the individual receivables remain unaffected.

18   They would be valued at $180 – their NRV (net realisable value) complying with the prudence concept.

19   Accruals and prepayments include provisions and adjustments covered by the matching or accruals concept.

The concept ensures that income and costs are matched to the trading period in which they were generated or incurred and not when the income is received or the expenditure paid.

FINAL ACCOUNTS

20   (i)   The statement of profit or loss shows the financial performance of a business for a period of time. It reports the revenue earned and expenses incurred in the period.

        (ii)   The statement of financial position reports the overall financial position of a business at a particular date, by reporting the assets, liabilities and capital balances.

21   Items include:

- drawings
- interest on drawings
- salary
- share of profit.

A closing credit balance represents a partner's accumulated share of retained profits.

22 A partnership agreement includes the following issues:

- amount of capital to be introduced by partners
- how profits are to be shared between partners (this may be by reference to interest on capital, notional salaries and a residual profit share)
- drawings by partners and interest thereon
- agreed business activities, along with any specifically excluded activities
- procedure for resolving disputes
- arrangements for dissolution of the partnership on the death or retirement of partners.

23 The five steps to recognise revenue in the financial statements are as follows:

- identify the contract with a customer
- identify the performance obligations of the contract
- determine the transaction price
- allocate the transaction price to the performance obligations in the contract
- recognise revenue when (or as) the entity satisfies a performance obligation.

Section 4

ANSWERS TO OBJECTIVE TEST QUESTIONS

ACCOUNTING PRINCIPLES AND CONCEPTS

1 B

Financial statements should disclose all material items which are likely to affect the decisions of users.

2 D

Financial records should be maintained to enable the business owner to meet a range of uses, for both internal decision-making and to provide to external interested parties.

3 B

The *Framework* identifies two fundamental qualitative characteristics, relevance and faithful representation, together with a further four enhancing qualitative characteristics – comparability, verifiability, timeliness and understandability.

4 D

Consistent accounting treatment should be applied to transactions both within an accounting period, and from one accounting period to another.

5 C

6

	Statement of profit or loss	*Statement of financial position*
Expenses	Correct	
Equity		Correct

7

	Fundamental qualitative characteristic	Enhancing qualitative characteristic
Understandability		Correct
Faithful representation	Correct	

8

	Selected answer
Going concern	
Comparability	Correct
Timeliness	Correct
Relevance	

9

	Selected answer
Verifiability	Correct
Materiality	
Historical cost	
Understandability	Correct

10

	Selected answer
Relevance	Correct
Reliability	
Faithful representation	Correct
Verifiability	

11   B

12   A

13   B

Purchases should be recorded when the transaction takes place, which in this case is on receipt of the items. If a business waits until receipt of the invoice to record a purchase, there could be an opportunity for 'window dressing' of the accounts at the end of the year, by asking suppliers not to send in invoices until later.

14   D

Providing information to the general public considers the external perspective of maintaining financial records.

15   B

Enabling the proprietor to make investment decisions considers the internal perspective of maintaining financial records.

16   D

17

	Selected answer
To claim back the sales tax	Correct
To identify the goods bought	Correct
To record how much is owed to the supplier	Correct
To record how much is owed from the customer	

18   C

19   C

PRINCIPLES AND PROCESSES OF BASIC BOOKKEEPING

20   C

21   A

22   D

23   C

24   B

25

	Selected answer
Sales ledger	Correct
The petty cash book	
The non-current asset register	Correct
The purchase returns day book	

26   C

27   B

28   D

29

	Selected answer
Statement of financial position	
Bank statement	Correct
Statement of profit or loss	
Supplier statement	Correct

30   D

31   B

32   B

33   A

34   C

35   D

36   A

37   B

38   A

39   C

40   D

The trial balance does not guarantee that all transactions have been correctly posted to the correct ledger accounts, or that there will not be any errors contained within the ledger accounts. It will confirm, however, that an equal value of debits and credits has been posted into the ledger accounts.

41 **B**

The trial balance may contain errors within individual ledger accounts. It does not confirm the profit or loss for the accounting period. The proprietor's capital account balance at the end of the accounting period will be confirmed when the final accounts are produced.

42 **B**

43 **D**

THE PREPARATION OF JOURNALS AND LEDGER ACCOUNTS

44 **D**

The receivables account is debited with the total amount owed, including sales tax. The sales account is credited with the value of sales excluding sales tax. The tax on sales, which is payable to the government, is a liability and is credited to a sales tax account.

45 **C**

Returns inwards are sales returns from customers. They can be thought of as 'negative sales' or 'negative income', so we debit a returns inwards account. The returns reduce the amount owed by credit customers, so we credit the receivables account (reducing an asset = credit entry).

46 **A**

Option B is incorrect as it refers to debiting cash sales, instead of crediting cash sales. Cash received is recorded by debiting the bank account, so answers C and D must be incorrect. Also, settlement discount received relates to early settlement of trade payables, so that is a further error. If a credit customer takes settlement discount, it is accounted for by debiting the revenue account and crediting accounts receivable.

47 **D**

48 **C**

This is a transaction that records an increase in non-current assets (motor vehicle) and an increase in capital.

49 **D**

Before the debt was written off it would have been recognised in receivables (with or without a related allowance for doubtful debts). To remove the debt receivables will be credited and a charge for irrecoverable debts will be recognised in profit or loss.

50 **D**

Cash sales do not affect receivables. Discounts received affect payables, not receivables.

The allowance for receivables does not affect receivables, but specific irrecoverable debts written off do affect receivables.

Receivables account

	$		$
Opening balance b/d	42,750	Contra with payables	18,750
Sales (credit sales)	362,750	Irrecoverable debts w/off	8,640
		Bank (balancing figure)	333,785
		Closing balance c/d	44,325
	———		———
	405,500		405,500
	———		———
Balance b/d	44,325		

51 D

RECORDING TRANSACTIONS AND EVENTS

52 D

53 B

The balances provided in the question are correctly classified as follows:

	$	
Machinery at cost	85,800	non-current asset
Accumulated depreciation on machinery	21,750	reduction in non-current asset
Trade receivables	42,650	current asset
Receivables allowance	1,570	reduction in current asset
Bank overdraft	6,470	current liability
Inventory at 1 November 20X6	21,650	charge in profit or loss

The inventory at 31 October 20X7 of $22,300 is also a current asset.

Thus the total value of current assets is: $63,380 ($42,650 – $1,570 + $22,300)

54 $4,273

Opening accrual	$297	Credit
Payments made	$4,570	Debit
Balance at 31 October 20X7	$4,273	Debit

NB: There is no closing accrual or prepayment as the invoices cover the period up to the end of the financial year.

55 D

56 C

	$	
Receivables balance	78,600	
Less Irrecoverable amount	(600)	
	——————	
Revised balance	78,000	
	——————	
Allowance at 1.5% =	1,170	
Existing allowance	1,200	
Reduction	30	i.e. credit to profit or loss

57 D

The accounting equation is Assets = Capital + Liabilities. So, we can have:

Assets ($14,000) = Capital ($10,000) + Liabilities ($4,000)

58 D

Inventory costing $400 is sold for $1,000, giving a profit of $600. The sales tax on the sale will be $200.

	Cash	Inventory	Liabilities	Capital
	$	$	$	$
Start business	1,000			1,000
Buy inventory		800	800	
Sell inventory	1,200	(400)	200	600
	——————	——————	——————	——————
	2,200	400	1,000	1,600
	——————	——————	——————	——————

59 $1,500

	$
Closing capital	4,500
Opening capital	(10,000)
	——————
Decrease in net assets	(5,500)
Drawings: profit taken out	8,000
Capital introduced	(4,000)
	——————
Loss for the year	(1,500)
	——————

60   **$38,020**

Current liabilities are:	$
Trade payables	32,165
Bank overdraft	5,855
	38,020

61   **C**

The purchase return reduces the amount owed to Rawlings by $800 plus sales tax.

$800 + (10% × $800) = $880.00

62   **$3.800**

Sales tax account

	$		$
Payables/bank (input sales tax)	6,000	Balance b/d	3,400
		Receivables/bank	
Bank	2,600	(output sales tax)	9,000
Balance c/d	3,800		
	12,400		12,400
		Balance b/d	3,800

Tax on sales (outputs) = 15% × $60,000 = $9,000

Tax on purchases (inputs) = (15/115) × $46,000 = $6,000

63   **$3,045**

The only item of current liabilities in the list is 'payables', which are $3,045.

64   **$3,000**

Non-current assets in the list are motor vehicles and fixtures and fittings, which are:

$2,400 + 600 = $3,000

65   **$2,732**

$18,955 − 11,334 − 2,447 − 664 − 456 − 120 −146 − 276 − 665 − 115 = $2,732

66   **A**

Closing inventory is debited to the inventory account, and is the opening balance for the start of the next period. Closing inventory also reduces the cost of sales, and so is credited to the statement of profit or loss.

67   D

The statement of financial position is a list of balances, not an account. Therefore no double entry is required.

68   A

The series of transactions might be recorded as follows:

Original purchase: Debit Purchases, and Credit Brad (accounts payable)

On payment: Debit Brad (accounts payable) and Credit Bank

Therefore, on cancellation of the cheque: Debit Bank, and Credit Returns outwards

69   B

A bank overdraft represents money owed to the bank. Legally it is repayable on demand and so it is classified as a current liability.

70 $74,890

	$
Opening capital	68,920
Add profit for the year	22,860
Less drawings in the year	(16,890)
	————
Closing capital	74,890
	————

71   C

The loan is a liability; this is shown as a credit in the statement of financial position.

The cash in hand is an asset; this is shown as a debit in the statement of financial position.

Assets and liabilities must be shown separately; they can only be netted-off if there is a legal right of off-set.

72 $19,000

Sales of $150,000 at a margin of 20% = a gross profit of $30,000.

Therefore cost of sales is $120,000 ($150,000 – $30,000)

Cost of sales =	Opening inventory +	Purchases –	Closing inventory, thus:
$120,000 =	$12,500 +	$126,500 –	$19,000 (balancing figure)

73 $34,050

Increase in capital is $8,286. This represents profit less drawings.

Therefore, profit is $8,286 + $25,764 = $34,050.

74   C

Assets will be increased by the purchase of the computer, and liabilities will be increased by the new loan.

75   C

Property repairs are a revenue expense. As this has been incorrectly treated as capital expenditure, expenses are understated (and therefore profit is overstated) and assets are overstated.

76 $40,191

Capital	=		$
		Non-current assets	33,750
	+	Inventory	4,845
	+	Trade receivables	11,248
	−	Trade payables	(9,633)
	−	Bank overdraft	(539)
	+	Prepayment	520
			———
			40,191
			———

77   D

78   C

Provision required	$7,634
Provision brought forward	$6,548
Increase in provision	$1,086 increase in provision = charge

79 $17,649

	$
Inventory	5,754
Trade receivables	11,745
Cash at bank	150
	———
	17,649
	———

80   A

Invoices	$4,728	Dr
Opening accrual	$353	Cr
Closing balance	$4,375	Dr

81   C

Balance per ledger	$31,554	Cr
Discount	$53	Dr
Invoice	$622	Cr
	———	
Corrected balance	$32,123	
	———	

82   D

83   D

84 $72,185

	$
Inventory	25,700
Trade receivables	48,325
Receivables allowance	(1,840)
	———
	72,185
	———

85 $45,100

	$
Trade payables	38,975
Bank overdraft	6,125
	———
	45,100
	———

86   C

	$
Accrual b'fwd	(327)
Amounts paid in the year	8,750
	———
Expense (debit balance)	8,423
	———

87   D

This entry will reduce receivables by the amount written off as irrecoverable.

88   C

	$
Receivables b'fwd	83,200
Less: irrecoverable w/off	(1,825)
	81,375
Allowance required	6,510
Allowance b/fwd	8,200
Reduction in allowance	1,690

i.e. a credit (next to Reduction in allowance 1,690)

89   B

90 $7,100

	$
Opening capital	18,000
Capital introduced	6,000
Drawings	(10,000)
Loss for the year – bal fig	**(7,100)**
Closing capital	6,900

91 $672.00

92 $5,675

	$
Opening liability	(4,275)
Paid in year	4,100
Output tax $90,000 @20%	(18,000)
Input tax $75,000 @ 20/120	12,500
Closing liability	(5,675)

93   B

	$
Trade payables	3,115
Bank overdraft	350
	3,465

94 $8,200

	$
Motor vehicles	7,200
Fixtures and fittings	1,000
	8,200

95 $3,260

	$	$
Sales		21,370
Cost of sales		(12,413)
Gross profit		8,957
Less: expenses		
Salaries and wages	3,560	
Motor expenses	572	
Rent and rates (600 + 150)	750	
Lighting and heating	702	
Sundry expenses	113	(5,697)
Profit for the year		3,260

96   D

	$
Inventory	5,243
Receivables	6,715
Cash at bank	115
	12,073

97   D

98 $583,000

	$	$
Balance b/fwd	84,700	
Credit sales – bal fig	583,000	
Cash received re credit sales		564,250
Contra with payables		8,300
Irrecoverable receivables		12,650
Balance c/fwd		82,500
	_____	_____
Profit for the year	667,700	667,700
	_____	_____

Note that the allowance for receivables is not relevant when preparing a trade receivables control account. It is accounted for as a separate item.

99   C

100 $18,000

	$	$
Sales		180,000
Cost of sales:		
Opening inventory	20,000	
Purchases	160,000	
Less: closing inventory – bal fig	(18,000)	(162,000)
	_____	_____
Gross profit 10% of sales		18,000
		_____

101 $23,832

	$
Opening capital	89,627
Profit for the year	32,678
Less: drawings - bal fig	(23,832)
	_____
Closing capital	98,473
	_____

102   B

If an item has been wrongly accounted for as a revenue expense, it means that profit for the year will be reduced i.e. understated. It also means that the amount should be added to the value of assets on the statement of financial position. Until the adjustment is made, assets will also be understated.

103 **$38,921**

	$
Non-current assets	33,750
Inventory	4,845
Trade receivables	11,248
Trade payables	(9,633)
Bank overdraft	(539)
	39,671
Less: accrual	(750)
	38,921

104 **C**

105 **$10,250**

	$
Balance 1 January 20X5	10,250
Profit for the year	8,500
Capital introduced	3,800
Drawings	(7,300)
Balance 31 December 20X5	15,250

106 **$55,842**

	$
Trade receivables	55,742
Petty cash	100
	55,842

107 **C**

Trade discount is always deducted when calculating the amount invoiced by the seller. In addition, as Smith is not expected to take account of the early settlement discount terms, the amount of revenue receivable is calculated after deduction of trade discount only $950. ($1000 × 95%). When Smith subsequently pays early to be eligible for the discount, the accounting entries should reflect that fact and record settlement of the amount outstanding and also a reduction in revenue.

Debit Cash $912 ($950 × 96%), Debit Revenue $38 ($950 × 4%), and Credit Trade receivables $950.

108 B

Trade discount is always deducted when calculating the amount invoiced by the seller. In addition, as Jones is expected to take account of the early settlement discount terms, the amount of revenue receivable is calculated after deduction of both trade discount and early settlement discount, a total of $2,280 ($2,500 × 95% × 96%). When Jones subsequently pays early to be eligible for the discount, the accounting entries should reflect the receipt of cash and clearance of the trade receivable for the amount expected.

Debit Cash $2,280 and Credit Trade receivables $2,280.

109 D

Trade discount is always deducted when calculating the amount invoiced by the seller. In addition, as Black is expected to take account of the early settlement discount terms, the amount of revenue receivable is calculated after deduction of both trade discount and early settlement discount, a total of $4,104 ($4,500 × 95% × 96%). When Black subsequently pays outside of the settlement discount period, the full amount of the receivable after trade discount of $4,275 ($4,500 × 95%) is due. The additional cash received in excess of the receivable amount of $171 is therefore accounted for as receipt of additional revenue.

Debit Cash $4,275, Credit Revenue $171, and Credit Trade receivables $4,104.

110 A

Trade discount is always deducted when calculating the amount invoiced by the seller. In addition, as White is not expected to take account of the early settlement discount terms, the amount of revenue receivable is calculated after deduction of trade discount only, a total of $3,515 ($3,700 × 95%). When White subsequently pays outside of the settlement discount period as expected, the full amount of the receivable is due.

111 A

Trade discount is always deducted when calculating the amount invoiced by the seller. In addition, as Green is expected to take account of the early settlement discount terms, the amount of revenue receivable is calculated after deduction of trade discount and early settlement discount, a total of $1,276.80 ($1,400 × 96% × 95%). When Green subsequently pays outside of the settlement discount period, the full amount of $1,344 ($1,400 × 96%) is due and the additional amount received of $67.20 ($1,344.00 - $1,276.80) is accounted for as receipt of additional revenue.

Debit Cash $1,344.00, Credit Revenue $67.20, and Credit Trade receivables $1,276.80.

INVENTORIES

112   B

113 $40,755

	$	$
Cost of inventory		41,875
Damaged items:		
Cost	1,960	
Expected sale value	1,200	
Less cost of repairs	360	
Net realisable value	840	
Write down ($1,960 – $840)		1,120
Inventory valuation		40,755

114 $3,567

Closing inventory is 160 units. Using FIFO, 150 of these are all deemed to be part of the final delivery, and therefore they are valued at $22.30 per unit = $3,345. The remaining 10 units are deemed to be part of the previous delivery and are therefore valued at $22.20 per unit = $222.

Thus total value is $3,567

115 $3,648

	Units	Unit cost $	Total cost $
Opening inventory	60	22.00	1,320.00
14 Aug Purchase	120	22.50	2,700.00
26 Aug Purchase	150	23.36	3,504.00
	330		7,524.00

Periodic weighted average cost per unit = $7,524.00/330 units = $22.80. Inventory valuation = 330 units – 170 sold = 160 × $22.80 = $3,648.00.

116 C

	Units	Unit cost $	Total cost $
Opening inventory	60	22.00	1,320.00
14 Feb Purchase	180	23.00	4,140.00
	240	22.75	5,460.00
18 Feb Sale	(90)	22.75	(2,047.50)
Closing inventory	150	22.75	3,412.50

Note that, using the continuous weighted average method of inventory valuation, a new weighted average cost per unit is calculated following each purchase made.

117 $6,825

	Units	Unit cost $	Total cost $
Opening inventory	120	22.00	2,640.00
15 Apr Purchase	360	23.00	8,280.00
	480	22.75	10,920.00
25 Apr Sale at cost	(300)	22.75	(6,825.00)
Closing inventory	180	22.75	4,095.00

Note that, using the continuous weighted average method of inventory valuation, a new weighted average cost per unit is calculated following each purchase made. The updated weighted average cost per unit is then used for each sale until the next purchase is made and the process is repeated.

118 $500

Inventory should be valued at the lower of cost and net realisable value. Net realisable values $1,200 – $250 = $950, with cost of $500 the lower of the two possibilities.

119 C

	$
Value at 7 July 20X6	38,950
Sales since year end (100/125 × $6,500)	5,200
Purchase since year end	(4,250)
Value at 30 June 20X6	39,900

120 A

The net realisable value of inventory items is the selling price less the 4% commission payable.

	NRV	Lower of cost or NRV
	$	$
Henry VII	2,784	2,280
Dissuasion	3,840	3,840
John Bunion	1,248	1,248
		7,368

121 D

The closing inventory of 12 items (15 – 5 + 10 – 8) comprise

	$
10 items at $3.50 each	35.00
2 items at $3 each	6.00
Cost on a FIFO basis is	41.00

122 B

The damaged items have a cost of $3,660, but a net realisable value of only $1,050 ($1,500 – $450). Therefore the cost of the inventory needs to be written down by $2,610 ($3,660 – $1,050). The inventory will then have a correct value of $36,140 ($38,750 – $2,610).

123 B

124 D

Closing inventory reduces the cost of sales figure. Therefore if the value of closing inventory is increased, cost of sales will be reduced and net profit will be increased. Net assets will also be increased.

125 B

The over-valuation in 20X4 will boost profits in 20X4 by reducing cost of sales. However, the opening inventories in the following year will be overstated increasing cost of sales and reducing profits.

126 $15,800

Inventories are valued at the lower of cost and net realisable value. The cost of repairing the clock will reduce the expected profit, but the clock's net realisable value is still greater then cost and so no reduction in value is needed.

127 $9.4M

$6.5m + $1.6m + $1.3m = $9.4m

128 C

Administrative costs are not included in the statement of financial position valuation of an item in the inventory.

129 B

130 $12.50

Assuming that all the costs would be incurred by the seller (and not the customer) the net realisable value is $20 – $2 – $3 – $2.50 = $12.50.

131 $87,700

	$
Payments for purchases	85,400
Less: Invoices for opening inventory	(1,700)
Plus: Invoices due for fuel purchased	1,300
Purchases	85,000

	$
Opening inventory	12,500
Purchases	85,000
Closing inventory	(9,800)
Cost of fuel – profit or loss	87,700

132 $4,700

	Net realisable value $	Lower of cost or NRV $	Units	Value $
Basic	8	6	200	1,200
Super	8	8	250	2,000
Luxury	10	10	150	1,500
Total value				4,700

133 B

With FIFO, closing inventory is the most recently purchased items, therefore when prices are rising, closing inventory will have a higher value than if the average cost method of inventory valuation is used. Since closing inventories will be valued higher, the cost of sales will be lower and the profit will be higher.

134 $21,510

22,960 – 1,950 – 400 + 900 = $21,510

135 $22,030

22,700 – 1,300 + 700 – 70 = $22,030

136 C

137 $3,420

Continuous average cost per unit = ($815+= (270 × $19.50))/320 units = $19.00. Therefore cost of goods sold = 180 × 180 units = $3,420.

NON-CURRENT ASSETS AND DEPRECIATION

138 D

If a business is a going concern, it is reasonable to assume that non-current assets will be used over their expected useful economic life. It is therefore appropriate to value a non-current asset at cost less accumulated depreciation, which represents the consumption of value so far.

139 C

Depreciation spreads the value of a non-current asset over its expected useful life.

140 B

Year 1 charge = $100,000 × 20% = $20,000, leaving a book value of $80,000.

Year 2 charge = $80,000 × 20% = $16,000.

141

	Selected answer
To calculate the total balance outstanding on loans raised to purchase non-current assets	
To help in carrying out the physical verification of non-current assets	Correct
To calculate the profit or loss on disposal of non-current assets	Correct
To eliminate the need to maintain ledger accounts relating to non-current assets	

142

	Selected answer
Cost of staff training to use the new plant and equipment	
Installation costs	Correct
Three-year maintenance agreement	
Delivery costs	Correct

Delivery and installation costs are incurred in getting the asset into working condition, and so they are capitalised. The maintenance costs merely maintain the asset, they do not improve it. Staff training costs can never be capitalised. Therefore they are charged as revenue expenditure.

143 $87,500

	$
Net book value of assets at start of year (140,000 – 60,000)	80,000
Assets purchased in the year	30,000
	110,000

	$
Depreciation at 25% of this balance: charge for the year	27,500
Opening balance, accumulated depreciation	60,000
Therefore closing balance	87,500

144 D

A non-current asset register is a detailed schedule of non-current, and is not another name for non-current asset ledger accounts in the general ledger.

145 A

The general ledger account for non-current assets shows a net book value that is $10,000 higher than the figure in the non-current assets register. This could be due to having omitted to deduct an asset with a NBV of $10,000 from the ledger. A non-current asset will have a NBV on disposal when it is sold for $15,000 and the profit on disposal is $5,000.

146 D

	$	
Proceeds	4,430	
Less carrying amount (12,000 – 5,856)	(6,144)	
	1,714	loss

147 $3,200

The total cost of the asset is $16,000 ($11,570 cash plus the $4,430 trade-in allowance). $16,000 × 20% = $3,200.

148

	15% straight-line	15% reducing balance
Asset 1		Correct
Asset 2	Correct	

Asset 1 – ($100,000 - $50,000) × 15% = $7,500 calculated using the reducing balance basis.

Asset 2 – ($50,000 × 15%) = $7,500 calculated using the straight-line basis.

149 A

150 $1,984

Year ended	Depreciation	Carrying amount c/f
31 October 20X4	$15,500 × 20% = $3,100	$15,500 – $3,100 = $12,400
31 October 20X5	$12,400 × 20% = $2,480	$12,400 – $2,480 = $9,920
31 October 20X6	$9,920 × 20% 1= $1,984	

151 D

152 D

Cost $80,000 and depreciation at 15% pa straight line is $12,000

A full year's depreciation will be charged in the years to 30 September 20X5, 20X6 and 20X7. Therefore, the carrying amount is $44,000. If proceeds are $39,000, there will be a loss of $5,000

153 $50,600

	$
Cost of plant	48,000
Delivery	400
Modifications	2,200
	50,600

154 B

		$
Year 1	Cost	2,400.0
	Depreciation at 20%	(480.0)
Year 2	Carrying value	1,920.0
	Depreciation at 20%	(384.0)
Year 3	Carrying value	1,536.0
	Depreciation at 20%	(307.2)
Year 4	Carrying value	1,228.8
	Sale proceeds	1,200.0
	Loss on disposal	(28.8)

155 $118,000

	$	$
Original balance		125,000
Carrying amount of asset sold:		
Proceeds	9,000	
Less: Profit	(2,000)	
		(7,000)
Adjusted balance		118,000

156 $360

	$
Cost	5,000
Year 1 (20% × 5,000)	(1,000)
Year 2 (20% × 4,000)	(800)
Year 3 (20% × 3,200)	(640)
Carrying amount at time of disposal	2,560
Sale proceeds	2,200
Loss on disposal	360

157 D

	Selected answer
The purchase of a car for a member of the sales department to visit clients	
The purchase of a car for resale by a car dealer	Correct
Legal fees incurred on the purchase of a building	
The cost of painting a building	Correct

The purchase of a car for resale means that the car is an item of inventory for the business, not a non-current asset. Legal fees incurred in purchasing a building are included in the cost of the building, and so is part of the non-current asset cost, i.e. capital expenditure. The cost of maintenance (i.e. painting a building) is a revenue expense. The cost of purchasing a car for use by an employee performing their work duties should be capitalised.

158 $200

Disposals account

	$		$
Cost	12,000	Accumulated depreciation (3 yrs × 20% × $12,000)	7,200
Profit (β)	200	Proceeds (part-exchange allowance)	5,000
	———		———
	12,200		12,200
	———		———

159 B

If an amount has been wrongly capitalised, rather than treated as an expense, the profit for the year will be higher than it should be. In addition, assets are overstated as they include an amount that should not have been capitalised.

160 C

If an amount has been wrongly accounted for as an expense, rather than capitalised, the profit for the year will be lower than it should be. In addition, assets are understated as they exclude an amount that should have been capitalised and accounted for as a non-current asset.

161 $6,000

Disposals account

	$		$
Cost	100,000	20X2 dep'n (100,000 × 20%)	20,000
Profit (β)	6,000	20X3 dep'n (800,000 × 20%)	16,000
		Disposal proceeds	70,000
	———		———
	106,000		106,000
	———		———

162 $6,250

Disposals account

		$			$
	Cost	100,000		20X2 dep'n (90,000 × 15%)	15,000
				20X3 dep'n (90,000 × 15%)	15,000
				20X4 dep'n (90,000 × 15% × 3/12)	3,750
				Disposal proceeds	60,000
				Loss on disposal (β)	6,250
		100,000			100,000

163 $90,800

Depreciation

		$			$
	Disposal	17,200	1/1/X7	Bal b/d	92,000
31/12/X7	Bal c/d	90,800	31/12/X7	Profit or loss statement	16,000
		108,000			108,000
			1/1/X8	Bal b/d	90,800

164 $2,000

Disposal

		$			$
	Cost	20,000		Dep'n	17,200
31/12/X7	Profit or loss	2,000		Bank	4,800
		22,000			22,000

165 $16,000

Cost

		$			$
1/1/X7	Bal b/d	180,000		Disposal	20,000
			31/12/X7	Bal c/d	160,000
		180,000			180,000

NCA Cost $160,000 × 10% = $16,000 = depreciation charge

166 D

The answer does not include all the required double entries, which are:

- Debit Disposal account, credit Machinery account ($20,000)
- Debit Accumulated depreciation, credit Disposal account ($17,200)
- Debit Cash, credit Disposal account ($4,800).

This leaves a balance on the account, representing the profit on disposal.

167 C

The gain or loss on disposal is the difference between the disposal value of the asset and its net book value at the date of disposal. If the asset's life and disposal value had been forecast with 100% accuracy, there would be no gain or loss on disposal.

168 $510,000

	Cost	Accum dep'n	CA
	$000	$000	$000
Opening balance	860	397	
Disposal	(80)	(43)	
	780	354	
Purchase	180		
Depreciation (10%)	960	96	
		450	
Carrying amount = 960 – 450			510

169 B

	$
Cost of asset	126,000
Depreciation to 31 October 20X3 (4/12 × 15%)	6,300
	119,700
Depreciation to 31 October 20X4 (15%)	17,955
	101,745
Depreciation to 31 October 20X5 (15%)	15,262
	86,483
Depreciation to 31 October 20X6 (15%)	12,972
	73,511
Depreciation to 30 September 20X7 (11/12 × 15%)	10,108
Net carrying amount at time of disposal	63,403
Disposal price	54,800
Loss on disposal	8,603

170 $1,836

Do not include the road tax in the cost of the car. Road tax is a revenue expense item.

	$
Cost of asset	10,000
Depreciation 20X1 (25%)	2,500
	7,500
Depreciation 20X2 (25%)	1,875
	5,625
Depreciation 20X3 (25%)	1,406
	4,219
Depreciation 20X4 (25%)	1,055
Net book value at time of disposal	3,164
Disposal value	5,000
Profit on disposal	1,836

171 $150,000

The asset disposed of had a net book value at the time of disposal = sales proceeds + loss on sale = $25,000 + $5,000 = $30,000.

	$
Carrying amount at 1 August 20X2	200,000
Carrying amount of asset disposed of	30,000
	170,000
Depreciation charge	20,000
Carrying amount at 31 July 20X3	150,000

172 A

You need to know the sales proceeds to calculate the length of ownership, or you need to know the length of ownership to calculate the sales proceeds. For example, this asset might have been sold after one year (NBV = $10,000) for $5,500, or it might have been sold after two years (NBV $8,000) for $3,500, and so on.

173 $87

	$
Cost of asset	9,000
Depreciation Year 1 (30%)	2,700
	6,300
Depreciation Year 2 (30%)	1,890
	4,410
Depreciation Year 3 (30%)	1,323
Net book value at time of disposal	3,087
Disposal value	3,000
Loss on disposal	87

174 $100

	$
Sale value	5,300
Carrying amount (10,000 – 4,800)	5,200
	100

175 D

		$
Cost		14,900
Less:	Accumulated depreciation	8,940
=	Net book value	5,960
	Proceeds	7,455
=	Profit	1,495

176 B

177 A

178 A

	Profit on disposal	*Loss on disposal*
Asset 1	Correct	
Asset 2		Correct

Asset 1: $7,500 - ($15,000 - $8,500) = $1,000 profit.

Asset 2: $6,500 − ($17,000 - $9,500) = $1,000 loss.

ACCRUALS AND PREPAYMENTS

179 $858,600

Rental income

	$		$
Balance b/f	42,300	Balance b/f	102,600
Statement of profit or loss (β)	**858,600**	Cash received	838,600
Balance c/f	88,700	Balance c/f	48,400
	———		———
	989,600		989,600
	———		———

180 A

		$
Statement of profit or loss	9/12 × $10,800	8,100
	3/12 × $12,000	3,000
		———
		11,100
		———
Statement of financial position prepayment	9/12 × $12,000	9,000

181 D

Statement of profit or loss (5/12 × $24,000) + (7/12 × $30,000) = $27,500

Statement of financial position $7,500 paid on 1 January therefore amount prepaid by tenant is:

2/3 × $7,500 = $5,000. For Vine this is prepaid/deferred income, i.e. income received in advance – a liability.

182 $385

Motor expenses

	$		$
Balance b/f (insurance)	80	Balance b/f (petrol)	95
Cash paid – petrol	95		
– other bills	245	**Statement of profit or loss (β)**	**385**
Balance c/f (petrol)	120	Balance c/f (insurance)	60
	———		———
	540		540
	———		———

The insurance prepayment covers 4 months as at the start of September. Therefore there must be a prepayment of 3 months at the end of September.

183 A

Charge to statement of profit or loss $1,800 × 7/12 = $1,050

Prepayment $1,800 × 5/12 = $750

184 C

The accrual for May and June 20X3 is assumed to be 2/3 × $840 = $560.

Electricity expenses

	$		$
Bank	600	Opening balance b/f	300
Bank	720		
Bank	900		
Bank	840		
Closing balance c/f	560	Statement of profit or loss	3,320
	———		———
	3,620		3,620
	———		———

185 B

The charge in the statement of profit or loss will be the amount of interest incurred from 1 January (when the loan was taken out) to 30 September (the year-end) i.e. 9/12 × 12% × $100,000 = $9,000. This represents three interest payments.

However, as only two interest payments were made (1 April and 1 July) the third payment due to be made on 1 October, which relates to the three months to 30 September, will be accrued: 3/12 × 12% × $100,000 = $3,000.

186 C

	$
Prepayment brought forward at the start of the year	10,000
Payment during the year	36,000
	46,000
Less: Prepayment carried forward at the year end (7 months, therefore $36,000 × 7/12)	(21,000)
Charge for insurance in the statement of profit or loss	25,000

187 A

Accrued income is income not yet received for a service already provided (income received in arrears). Accounting for accrued income will therefore increase, rather than decrease, profit. A prepayment is an asset and an accrual is a liability.

188 B

The charge in the statement of profit or loss will be the amount of interest incurred from 1 January (when the loan was taken out) to 31 March (the year-end) i.e. 3/12 × 10% × $250,000 = $6,250. This represents three months of accrued interest charges due to be paid on 1 April 20X3. This will also be the accrual in the statement of financial position as no payment has been made in the period to 31 March 20X3.

189 A

Tutorial note

- *The reduction in cash is replaced by an increase in prepayments and therefore assets remain unchanged.*

- *Liabilities are not affected and so remain unchanged.*

- *As Capital = Assets – Liabilities and both assets and liabilities remain unchanged, it remains that capital is unchanged.*

190 C

Rent of $7,800 paid in advance, thus prepayment at year end. At 30 November, two months of the period for which rent has been paid is unexpired.

Rent for one month = $7,800 ÷ 4 = $1,950

Two months paid in advance = $1,950 × 2 = $3,900

191 $1,813

Electricity account

	$		$
Paid in year	1,765	Opening balance	264
Closing balance	312	Charge for year	1,813 (bal fig)
	———		———
	2,077		2,077
	———		———

192 $1,268

The opening balance will represent the accrual of $1,268.

As this is an accrual (or liability), the opening trial balance will record a credit balance.

193 C

The cash paid during the year is indicated by the bank transactions (3,000 + 3,000 + 3,600 + 3,600 = 13,200). The charge to profit or loss is shown as $13,000.

194 C

	$
5 months at ($24,000/12) per month	10,000
7 months at ($30,000/12) per month	17,500
	———
Annual rent expense	27,500
	———

195 A

Charge to the profit or loss:

7 months: $7/12 \times \$1,800 = \$1,050$

Prepayment of rent:

5 months: $5/12 \times \$1,800 = \$750$

196 C

Profit or loss charge for insurance:

(7 months): $7/12 \times \$2,400 = \$1,400$

Prepayment: 5 months = $5/12 \times \$2,400 = \$1,000$

197 $3,300

The situation in the question is unusual because there is an opening accrual on the account, but a closing prepayment of 1/3 × $1,200 = $400.

Rent account

	$		$
Bank	4,000	Balance b/d (accrual)	300
		Profit or loss statement	3,300
		Balance c/d (prepayment)	400
	———		———
	4,000		4,000
	———		———

198 C

The accrual for May and June 20X3 is assumed to be 2/3 × $840 = $560.

Electricity expenses account

	$		$
Bank	600	Opening balance b/d	300
Bank	720		
Bank	900		
Bank	840		
Closing balance c/d	560	Profit or loss statement	3,320
	———		———
	3,620		3,620
	———		———
		Opening balance b/d	560

199 $12,600

Insurance for the year 1 July 20X2 to 30 June 20X3 was $13,200 × 1/1.1 = $12,000.

Profit or loss charge:

Six months at $12,000 plus six months at $13,200 = $6,000 + $6,600.= $12,600

200 $1,840

The rent payment covers the period 1 March to 31 August. At 30 June, there is a prepayment of two months (July and August). The amount of the prepayment is 2/6 × $5,520 = $1,840.

201 $1,400

There is an accrual for two months (October and November) during which electricity charges have been incurred but no invoice has been received yet. The best estimate of the accrual is 2/3 × $2,100 = $1,400.

202 B

A prepaid expense will reduce the charge to profit or loss. It will also be shown as a current asset in the statement of financial position.

203 C

The accrual should have been for $700, but was actually $1,400. Therefore it needs to be reduced by $700.

204 B

	$
Loss reported in draft accounts	(1,486)
Less accrual (an additional expense)	(1,625)
Add back prepayment (a reduction in expenses)	834
Revised loss	(2,277)

205 D

Under the accruals concept, the accounts should include the cost of electricity consumed up to the end of the financial year. The charge for the last two months should be estimated, and included in the charge against profit. The best available estimate is based on the last bill, which indicates a monthly charge of $1,090. Thus the total accrual is $2,180.

206 B

The opening trial balance will reflect the liability brought forward. (The charge to profit or loss has been written off, and is therefore eliminated from the expense account.)

207

	Accrual	Prepayment
Repairs and renewals		Correct
Light and heat	Correct	

Repairs and renewals: $39,500 - $2,000 - $36,500 = $1,000 prepayment.

Light and heat: $25,000 - $1,000 - $25,500 = $1,500 accrual.

IRRECOVERABLE DEBTS AND ALLOWANCES FOR RECEIVABLES

208 $5,350

	$	Allowance $	Expense $
Receivables balance (draft)	58,200		
Irrecoverable debts	(8,900)		8,900
	49,300		
Specific allowance: Carroll	(1,350)	1,350	
Juffs	(750)	750	
	47,200		
Allowance c/f		2,100	
Allowance b/f		5,650	
Decrease in allowance		3,550	(3,550)
Total expense			5,350

209 $13,450

Receivables' ledger control account

	$		$
Balance b/f (W)	13,150		
Sales	125,000	Cash	115,500
		Irrecoverable debts	7,100
		Balance c/f	15,550
	138,150		138,150

	b/f $	c/f $
Gross receivables	13,150	15,550
Allowance	(1,150)	(2,100)
Net receivables	12,000	13,450

210 B

The write off of debts will reduce the gross receivables balance by $72,000 to $766,000.

The allowance is to be adjusted to $60,000 (hence an adjustment of $12,000).

The net balance is therefore $766,000 less $60,000, i.e. $706,000.

211 $5,083

Year-end receivables	5% × $7,000,000	=	$350,000
Year-end allowance for receivables		=	$14,000
Allowance at start of year		=	$11,667
Increase in allowance		**=**	**$2,333**

Note that the irrecoverable debts had been written off during the year and have already been excluded from the receivables balance at 30 September 20X8.

Irrecoverable debts expense

	$		$
Write off of irrecoverable debts	3,200	Recovery of irrecoverable debts	450
Increase in allowance	2,333	Statement of profit or loss (β)	5,083
	_____		_____
	5,533		5,533
	_____		_____

212 $20,200

Trade receivables

	$		$
Balance b/f	10,000	Receipts	90,000
Sales	100,000	Irrecoverable in year	800
Irrecoverable debts recovered	1,000	Balance c/f	20,200
	_____		_____
	111,000		111,000
	_____		_____

213 A

When a debt is written off as irrecoverable, the transaction is recorded as:

Dr Irrecoverable debts account (expense), and Cr Receivables' ledger control account

Any subsequent change to the allowance for receivables should be dealt with as a separate matter.

214 $340,750

Cash sales do not affect receivables.

Discounts received affect payables, not receivables.

The allowance for receivables does not affect the amount of receivables, but specific irrecoverable debts written off do affect receivables.

Receivables

	$		$
Balance b/f	37,500	Contra with payables	1,750
Sales (credit)	357,500	Irrecoverable debts written off	3,500
		Bank (β)	340,750
		Balance c/f	49,000
	———		———
	395,000		395,000
	———		———

215 $800

	$
Irrecoverable debts written off (800 + 550)	1,350
Irrecoverable debt recovered	(350)
Reduction in allowance for receivables	(200)
	———
Charge to statement of profit or loss	800
	———

216 B

The allowance for receivables will reduce the book value of receivables. An increase in an allowance for receivables will therefore reduce net current assets.

217 $5,270

	$	$
Receivables balance	230,000	
Specific allowance – Emily	(450)	450
– Lulu	(980)	980
– Sandy	(5,000)	5,000
	———	
	228,570	
		———
Total allowance at end of year c/f		6,430
Allowance b/f		(11,700)
		———
Decrease in allowance = Cr to statement of profit or loss		5,270

218 A

The net amount reported in the statement of financial position is $47,744 due less the $3,500 allowance for doubtful debts.

219 $2,000

The charge for irrecoverable debts and allowance for receivables is the actual amount of bad debts written off plus the increase in the allowance for doubtful debts, or minus the decrease in the allowance.

	$
Allowance required at end of year	6,000
Allowance required at start of year	9,000
Decrease in allowance	(3,000)
Irrecoverable debts written off	5,000
Charge to profit or loss	2,000

220 $158

	$
Allowance required	5,512
Less: opening allowance	(5,670)
Decrease (credit) recognised in profit or loss	(158)

CAPITAL AND FINANCE COSTS

221 D

222 $7,000

	$
Capital balance b/fwd	12,000
Capital introduced in the year	1,500
Profit (loss) for the year **bal fig**	7,000
Drawings	(6,000)
Capital balance c/fwd	14,500

223 $23,000

	$
Capital balance b/fwd	12,000
Capital introduced in the year **bal fig**	23,000
Profit (loss) for the year	(13,000)
Drawings	(7,500)
Capital balance c/fwd	14,500

224 $15,300

	$
Capital balance b/fwd	23,000
Capital introduced in the year	3,000
Profit (loss) for the year	(2,500)
Drawings	(8,200)
	——————
Capital balance c/fwd **bal fig**	15,300
	——————

225 $9,600

	$
Capital balance b/fwd	35,000
Profit (loss) for the year **bal fig**	9,600
Drawings	(14,600)
	——————
Capital balance c/fwd	30,000
	——————

226 $41,650

	$
Capital balance b/fwd **bal fig**	41,650
Capital introduced in the year	2,750
Profit (loss) for the year	13,800
Drawings	(15,700)
	——————
Capital balance c/fwd	42,500
	——————

227 $7,700

	$
Capital balance b/fwd	12,735
Profit (loss) for the year **bal fig**	(7,700)
Drawings	(2,345)
	——————
Balance c/fwd	2,690
	——————

228 C

Liabilities should also include six months of interest accrued of $300 ($7,500 × 8% × 6/12).

229 **$15,000**

	$
Capital balance b/fwd	28,350
Capital introduced in the year	3,000
Profit (loss) for the year	9,335
Drawings **bal fig**	(15,000)
	———
Capital balance c/fwd	25,685
	———

230 **$14,750**

	$
Capital balance b/fwd	18,500
Capital introduced in the year **bal fig**	14,750
Profit (loss) for the year	(8,000)
Drawings	(8,500)
	———
Capital balance c/fwd	16,750
	———

231 **C**

CONTROL ACCOUNTS, RECONCILIATIONS AND ERRORS

232 **A**

233 **B**

234 **B**

The payables' ledger control account and the motor expenses account are posted from the PDB. Because the original entry in the PDB was overstated by $36 then both of the postings will also be overstated by $36 – this needs to be corrected

235 **$38,002**

The list of balances will be reconciled to the corrected ledger balance as follows:

	$		$
Total of list	37,552	Balance	38,842
Add Balance omitted	1,200	Less Error in daybook	90
	———		———
	38,752		38,752
Less Credit note	750	Less Credit note	750
	———		———
	38,002		38,002

236 D

237 D

238 C

239

	True	*False*
Control accounts can help to speed up the preparation of draft accounts by providing the statement of financial position values for trade receivables and trade payables	Correct	
Control accounts are always used in double entry bookkeeping		Correct

Control accounts are useful, but they are not essential. The double entry can be directly to individual supplier or customer accounts.

240 C

Listing a debit balance as a credit affects the list of balances but not the control account. The transposition error in the PDB will affect the totals posted to the control account.

241 D

This answer assumes that the individual supplier accounts are drawn up from the information in the PDB, rather than from the original invoices.

242 $36,676

$35,776 + $900 = $36,676. The error on the list of balances does not affect the control account, but the $900 undercast on the SDB needs to be adjusted.

243 A

The cancelled cheques should be entered in the bank account by debiting $642.

244 B

A debit entry of $1,300 is needed to correct the error: $650 to cancel out the incorrect credit and a further $650 to make the entry that should have been made.

245

	True	*False*
A separate suspense account should be opened for each error in the ledgers		Correct
A suspense account is sometimes opened to complete postings whilst more information is sought on a transaction.	Correct	

There is no need to open a separate suspense account for each error. Therefore the first statement is incorrect. A suspense account is sometimes used to complete a posting while further information is being sought, so the second statement is correct.

246 C

The suspense account balance will remain $280 as it is unaffected by the correction of the error. The entries needed to correct the error are debit supplier account and credit purchases with $140.

247 $75,355

The list of balances on the individual suppliers' accounts needs to be reduced by the invoice posted twice and the unrecorded payment. This will result in a figure of $75,355 ($81,649 – $4,688 – $1,606). The payables control account needs to be reduced by the unrecorded payment to $75,355 ($76,961 – $1,606).

248 C

$1,500 of purchases is being moved from stationery into purchases.

249 A

Total credit purchases have been added up wrongly and are too high, and the general ledger accounts have therefore recorded purchases, payables and input tax at too high an amount. To correct this error, we need to reduce purchases (credit purchases account), reduce payables (debit trade payables control account) and reduce input tax recoverable (credit sales tax account). The trade payables control account balance will be reduced by $4,000 to $175,000.

250 C

Here the error affects the individual supplier's account in the payables ledger, which is not part of the double entry system. To correct this, we need to reduce the balance on the account of H. As a result, the total of the balances on the supplier accounts in the payables ledger will be reduced by $1,000 to $175,000.

251 D

Discounts received from suppliers have been omitted from the accounts. To correct the error, they should be recorded. Discounts received are credited to a discounts received account. (As a form of income, discounts received are credited to the account.) The total amount payable to suppliers should be reduced, so debit the payables ledger control account. Amounts due to individual suppliers should also be reduced, by making adjustments in the accounts of the individual suppliers concerned, in the payables ledger.

252 $700

	$
Overdraft in bank statement	(38,600)
Deposits not yet credited to the account	41,200
	————
	2,600
Cheques paid but not yet presented to the bank	(3,300)
	————
Overdraft per cash book (credit balance)	(700)
	————

253

	Selected answer
Bank charges	Correct
Cheque not presented	
A dishonoured cheque from a customer	Correct
Deposits not credited	

An entry is required in the cash book for all correct items in the bank statement that have not yet been recorded in the cash book. These are the items that the business learns about when the bank statement has been received, and should then record those items in its own accounting records (i.e. initially in the cash book). Such items include bank charges (including overdraft interest) and details of dishonoured cheques. Cheques not yet presented and deposits not yet credited have already been recorded in the cash book.

254 B

In an imprest system, the money in petty cash is topped up to a maximum limit from time to time. This is done by drawing cash from the bank equal to the total of petty cash expenditure since the last time petty cash was topped up. (This amount should equal the total of the payments recorded on the petty cash vouchers that are in the petty cash box.)

255 D

The purchases day book has been undercast by $500 (i.e. the total is $500 lower than it should be). As a result of this, the purchases account has been debited and the payables' ledger control account (total payables) credited with $500 too little.

The sales day book has been overcast by $700. As a result, the sales account has been credited and the receivables' ledger control account (total receivables) has been debited with $700 too much.

As a result of these errors, the control account balances need to be adjusted, and profit reduced by ($500 + $700) $1,200, by reducing sales and increasing purchases.

Neither error affects the entries in the accounts of individual receivables and payables.

256 B

Error 1   Total sales and total receivables have been recorded $370 too much.

Error 2   Total cash receipts have been recorded ($940 – $490) $450 too little.

As a result of these two errors, credit entries to the receivables ledger control account need to be made totalling $820 ($370 + $450).

The errors do not affect the accounts of individual receivables.

257 A

As a result of the error, total payables are under-stated by $265,080 – 260,580 = $4,500. To correct the error, we need to increase the balance in the payables ledger control account, and this is done by crediting the control account.

The error has affected the control account only, and not the entries in the individual creditor accounts in the payables ledger, so the total of payables' balances is unaffected.

258 B

You think that you owe $150 more than the supplier has stated. With items A, C and D, the result would be that the supplier will state that you owe more, not less, than you think. If the supplier has recorded discount allowed to you, which you have not yet recorded, this will reduce the amount owed by you.

259 A

This is not an easy question to solve. You should prepare a receivables ledger control account and calculate the closing balance as a debit balance. You should then look for the answer that gives the same net debit balance. Here, the closing balance is $32,125, and only answer A gives this net amount.

Receivables ledger control account

	$		$
Opening balance b/d	32,750	Opening balance b/d	1,275
Sales	125,000	Bank	122,500
		Contra with payables	550
		Sales returns	1,300
		Closing balance (net)	32,125
	———		———
	157,750		157,750
	———		———
Opening balance (net)	32,125		

260 B

Neither of the statements is correct because if, for example:

(i)   a transaction has been omitted, or has been recorded incorrectly in both the general ledger and the personal account, the balance on the control account and the total of the list of balances will agree, but both will be incorrect

(ii) an error has been made in the general ledger only, the list of balances will be correct, but the ledger balance will be incorrect.

261 D

To correct the error, we need to reduce building repairs expenses (so credit Building repairs account) and we need to record the expense as an increase in motor vehicle repairs costs (so debit the Motor vehicle repairs account). (Remember! Expenses are debited to the appropriate expense account.)

262 D

With returns inwards, debit the sales returns account and credit the receivables account with in order to reduce the amount owed by the credit customer.

263 C

The debit entry is overstated by $180 because of this transposition error. The credit entry (to trade payables) is correct.

264 B

Only the incorrectly recorded cheque requires a correcting entry. The unpresented cheque is just a timing difference.

265 C

The correction to purchases will reduce the charge by $900, reducing the total debits by $900 and so increasing the suspense account needed to $1,800. Information about the missing cheque is sparse (is it income or an expense?) but it will have no effect on the suspense account if the transaction has been completely omitted from the TB.

266 D

The correct entry is:

Debit   Office cleaning expenses

Credit   Cash

Thus the entry in the trade payables account should be cancelled, and an entry is required in the cash account. The entry in the office cleaning expenses account must also be corrected.

267 $78,425

Only the discount not recorded will affect the balance on the payables' ledger control account. It is the corrected ledger control account balance which should be reported on the statement of financial position.

268 B

269 D

The corrected general ledger balance should be reported on the statement of financial position. In this case no adjustments are needed to the general ledger balance, as the reconciling items arise due to transactions being recorded at different times by the client and the bank (these are sometimes referred to as 'timing differences').

270 D

Tutorial note

Errors of transposition are taken to affect one side of the double entry only. Therefore the two sides of the double entry are not equal and so result in an imbalance of the trial balance.

271 **C**

> **Tutorial note**
>
> *The sales account entry should have been a credit of $3,450; instead it was a debit of $3,540. To correct the error, the debit entry must be reversed by crediting $3,540 and the correct entry recorded by crediting $3,450. The effect of both of these entries is to credit the sales account by $6,990. This will increase profit by $6,990, indicating that it was previously understated by the same amount.*

272 **A**

273 **A**

Opening balance on account	$420 debit
Cash sale omitted in sales account. A credit entry is required in the sales account. Thus the entry required in the suspense account is	$80 debit
Error has increased the credit balance by $700 and omitted a debit balance of $100. Thus the incorrect account requires a debit entry of $800, leading to a credit entry in the suspense account.	$800 credit
Thus closing balance	$300 credit

274 **C**

The ledger balance of $422 credit should be adjusted by a debit entry of $153 for interest. Thus the corrected balance is $269 credit.

The statement balance will therefore be an overdraft of $269 after the cheque of $822 has been processed.

Therefore the statement balance must currently be $553 cash at bank.

275 **D**

276 **$68,665**

Payables' ledger control account

	$		$
		Opening balance b/d	68,566
Closing balance c/d	68,665	Undercast purchases day book	99
	___		___
	68,665		68,665
	___		___
		Opening balance b/d	68,665

277 B

	$
Cash book balance (debit, therefore cash in the bank)	25,000
Items not yet in the bank statement:	
Payments to suppliers	3,500
Payments into the account (lodgements)	(3,800)
	———
Bank statement balance	24,700

278 C

	$
Overdraft per bank statement	(38,600)
Deposits not yet credited to the account	41,200
	———
	2,600
Cheques paid but not yet presented to the bank	(3,300)
	———
Overdraft in cash book	(700)

279 B

	$
Opening balance	(89.93)
Interest	(16.45)
	———
	(106.38)

280 C

	$
Cash book balance	148
Bank charges	(10)
Standing order	(25)
	——
Corrected cash book	113

	$
Cash book figure	113
Unpresented cheques	125
Outstanding lodgements	(85)
	——
	153

281 A

	$
Balance per bank statement	(210)
Less: unpresented cheques	(83)
Add: uncredited lodgements	30
	____
Corrected balance per cash book	(263)
	____

282 C

A credit in the bank statement is a debit entry in the cash book.

283 D

Reconciliations between the accounts receivable ledger and the trade receivables' ledger control account are carried out to check that the balance on the receivables' ledger control account equals the total of all the individual balances on the accounts receivable ledger. If a transaction has been posted to the account of the wrong customer in the accounts receivable ledger, the total of receivables balances is not affected. This error would not be discovered by the control account reconciliation.

284 A

As a result of the error, total payables are under-stated by $259,440 – $254,940 = $4,500. To correct the error, we need to increase the balance in the payables' ledger control account, and this is done by crediting the control account.

The error has affected the control account only and not the entries in the individual payable account for Figgins Co in the purchase ledger, so the total of payables' balances is unaffected.

285 B

BNO apparently owes ANO $150 more than the supplier statement identifies. With items, A, C and D the result would be that the supplier will state that you owe more, not less. Item B is the only possible answer which could explain the situation.

286 D

Receivables' ledger control account

	$		$
Opening balance	1,586		
SDB	100		
CB	100	Bal c/d	1,786
	_____		_____
	1,786		1,786
	_____		_____

287 A

Payables' ledger control account

	$		$
CB (14,576 – 14,756)	180	Opening bal	3,446
Receivables' ledger control account	392		
Closing bal	2,874		
	————		————
	3,446		3,446
	————		————

288 D

	$
Receivables' ledger total balances	50,000
Credit transfer (reduces receivables)	(750)
Contra entry (reduces receivables)	(2,000)
	————
Adjusted receivables' ledger balances	47,250
	————

289 D

Trade payables

	$		$
Cash paid re credit purchases	69,500	Balance b/d	23,450
Balance c/d	25,600	Purchases (bal fig)	71,650
	————		————
	95,100		95,100
	————		————

ADJUSTMENTS TO THE TRIAL BALANCE

290 B

291 D

292 B

This is an example of an irrecoverable debt being written off. This requires a credit to the receivables account in order to clear the debt and debit the bad debts account with the amount of the debt written off.

293 A

294 C

295 C

	$
Allowance required	890
Allowance brought forward	770
Increase	120

As the allowance has increased, a charge will be made to profit or loss.

296 A

Receivables (5% of $2 million) = $100,000.

Required allowance for receivables = $4,000.

Current allowance for receivables = $4,000 × ¾ = $3,000.

Increase in allowance = $1,000. An increase in the allowance for receivables reduces profit.

297 B

	$
Required allowance for receivables	3,600
Allowance last year ($3,600 × 100/125)	2,880
Increase in allowance	720
Irrecoverable debts written off	3,200
Irrecoverable debts recovered	(150)
Charge to profit or loss	3,770

298 C

	$
Allowance for receivables at start of year:	630
Required allowance at end of year	525
Reduction in allowance (credit profit or loss)	105

299 B

The receipt has been accounted for: Debit Bank, Credit Receivables' ledger control account.

It should have been accounted for as: Debit Bank, Credit Irrecoverable debts.

(The receivable was removed from the accounts when the irrecoverable debt was written off. The receipt is the recovery of an irrecoverable debt, which is credited to the irrecoverable debts account.)

To correct the error: Debit Receivables' ledger control account, Credit Irrecoverable debts.

300 B

	$
Irrecoverable debts written off	18,000
Reduction in allowance for receivables	(17,000)
	———
Net charge for irrecoverable debts and allowance for receivables	1,000
	———

A charge is an expense, which is a debit item.

301 B

Receivables balances	$37,890	
Less: write off	$1,570	
Revised receivables	$36,320	
Less: allowance req'd	$1,158	(i.e. allowance required at 30 Nov 20X6)
Net receivables in SOFP	$35,162	

302 C

303 C

Sybil still has to pay her phone bill for November and this must be reflected in her accounts.

(⅓ × $1,800) = $600 (accrued expenses)

304 D

The non-current assets (accumulated depreciation) account is a credit balance. The accounts receivable ledger control account should be a credit balance. The accounts payable ledger control account should have a credit balance.

305 C

If the bank interest and charges balance has been omitted, it should be included. Bank interest and charges is an expense and so it will be a debit balance. Complete the double entry by crediting the Suspense account.

306 A

Note (iv) states that the charge has been recorded in the Accumulated depreciation account, but has been omitted from the expense (cost of sales) account. Therefore debit cost of sales and credit suspense.

307 D

Under-casting the sales day book means that the total of credit sales has been recorded in the general ledger at too low an amount. To correct, we need to increase total receivables (so debit Accounts receivables ledger control) and increase Sales revenue (so credit sales account).

308 D

We need to eliminate the incorrect debit by crediting the administration account with $1,000 and crediting it with $1,000 again to make the entry that should have been made. The corresponding debit entry is to the Suspense account.

309 B

A suspense account is needed when, as a result of an accounting error, total credit balances and debit balances will not be equal to each other.

Error 1   The entry should have been Credit Bank, Debt Motor Vehicles account. Instead, it was recorded as Credit Bank, Credit Motor Vehicles account. A suspense account is needed.

Error 2   The entry should have been Debit Bank, Credit Brown, but was recorded as Debit Bank, Credit Green. Total credits and debits will be equal, so a suspense account is not needed to correct the error.

Error 3   The entry has been recorded as: Credit Bank $9,500, Debit Rent $5,900. Credits and debits are unequal, so a suspense account is needed to account for the correction required.

Error 4   The transaction has been recorded as Debit Payables, Credit Revenue, but should have been recorded as Debit Payables, Credit Discount received. Total credits and debits will be equal, so a suspense account is not needed to correct this error.

Error 5   An omission of a transaction does not need a suspense account to correct it.

310 C

Since total debits are less than total credits in the trial balance by ($1,026,480 − $992,640) $33,840, we need a debit balance of $33,840 in the suspense account to make the total debits and total credits equal.

Error 1   Does not affect the suspense account, because it is an omission and omissions do not alter debits and credits.

Error 2   Has treated a debit balance of $27,680 as a credit balance, as a result of which total credits will exceed total debits by 2 × $27,680 = $55,360.

Error 3   Does not affect the suspense account, since the error has been to debit the motor vehicle asset account instead of the bank account with $6,160.

Error 4   Has been to omit a credit balance of $21,520 for rent payable, as a result of which total debits will exceed total credits by $21,520.

To correct the errors:	$
Credit suspense account	55,360
Debit suspense account	21,520
	–––––––
To eliminate suspense account balance	33,840
	–––––––

311 C

This is a complex question. Remember that a suspense account is needed when, as a result of an accounting error, total credit balances and debit balances are not equal to each other.

Error 1 The original entry for the sales return would have been: Debit Sales returns, Credit Receivables. When the cash refund is paid, the entry should be Credit Cash, Debit Receivables. The error is really two errors. The wrong customer account has been used, but a debit entry has been recorded as a credit entry.

Error 5 The entry should have been Credit Bank, Debit Plant repairs, but has been Credit Bank, Credit Plant and equipment account. A suspense account is needed to correct this error.

Errors 2, 3 and 4 do not result in total debits and total credits being unequal.

Error 2 The wrong accounts have been used, but the debit entry and credit entry are equal. (The correct entry should be Credit Purchases, Debit Director's Current Account.)

Error 3 The entries made were Debit Irrecoverable debts, Credit Accumulated depreciation account, but should have been Debit Depreciation expense account, Credit Accumulated depreciation account. However, total debits and total credits are equal.

Error 4 These transactions were omitted from the accounting records.

312 A

Think of the other side of the double-entry that is needed to correct the error. This will help you to decide whether the entry in the suspense account should be a debit or a credit entry.

Error 1 To correct, we must debit gas account $180, therefore credit suspense account.

Error 2 To correct, we need to debit heat and light $50 and debit stationery $50, so we must credit the suspense account with 2 × $50.

Error 3 To correct, we need to credit interest receivable, therefore we debit the suspense account.

Suspense account

	$		$
Balance (balancing figure)	210	Gas expense	180
Interest received	70	Heat and light	50
		Stationery	50
	───		───
	280		280

313 D

314 D

Discounts received should be recorded as: Debit Payables and Credit Discounts received.

Here, the discount has been debited instead of credited, so that the balance in the discounts received account is 2 × $200 = $400 too low. To correct, we must therefore:

Credit Discounts received $400 and Debit Suspense account $400.

315 B

The wording of this question can make it quite difficult, but the correct answer might be identified quickly.

Item B   Discounts received should be credited, therefore there is no error. If there is no error, a suspense account entry is not required.

Item A   This is an error where a debit entry has been incorrectly recorded as a credit balance. A suspense account entry will be required to correct this.

Item C   This might cause you a problem. If the irrecoverable debt has been omitted entirely, and no accounting entry has been made, there can be no suspense account entry. Here, it would seem that the receivables balance has been reduced for the irrecoverable debt (credit Receivables) but the irrecoverable debt expense account has not recorded the bad debt. If so, credits exceed debits and a suspense account entry is needed.

Item D   The error in item D makes total debits higher by $180. These will therefore cause an entry in the suspense account.

316 A

To decide what entries are needed in the suspense account, you should think about the entry in the other account that is needed to correct the error. The entry in the suspense account is then the other side of the double entry. For example, inventory (an asset) should be a debit balance, so to correct the error, we need to debit the inventory account and credit suspense account. Similarly, sales tax payable should be a credit balance, and to record the missing sales tax, we need to credit the sales tax account, debit suspense account.

Suspense account			
	$		$
Balance (balancing figure)	2,050	Inventory (1,475 + 1,745)	3,220
Telephone expense (2 × $190)	380		
Sales tax ($5,390 – $4,600)	790		
	3,220		3,220

317 A

The sales tax balance for purchases should be a debit balance, because the money is recoverable from the tax authorities. The sales tax recoverable has been recorded as a credit entry (liability) instead of a debit entry, so to make the correction, we need to debit the sales tax account by 2 × $3,079 = $6,158. The correction is Debit sales tax $6,158, Credit Suspense account $6,158.

318 B

If the suspense account shows a credit balance, the correcting entry to clear the account must be Debit Suspense account $130, credit the account with the error $130.

Purchases have been over-stated by $130, and to correct this, we need to credit the Purchases account (and so debit Suspense account) with $130.

Omissions of transactions (item A and possibly item C) do not affect total debits and credits. If item C means that total receivables have been reduced by the bad debt, but the bad debts account does not yet show the bad debt, the correcting entry would be to debit the Bad debts account and credit Suspense account. The error in item D leaves total debits and credits equal.

319 $50,101

	$
Profit or loss statement credit balances (income)	281,917
Profit or loss statement debit balances (expenses)	231,816
	————
Profit for the year	50,101
	————

320 $12,081

The debit profit or loss column exceeds the credit column by $12,081. This means that expenses have exceeded income, so the business has made a loss.

321 C

The depreciation expense is charged (debited) to profit or loss.

The accumulated depreciation is a credit balance in the statement of financial position, reducing the carrying value of the related asset.

322 D

Items A and B would not create an imbalance because the mistakes affect both sides of the trial balance.

Item C would cause the credit side to be greater than the debit side.

Item D would cause the debit side to be overstated by $250 and the credit side to be understated by $250. This means that the debit side is $500 higher than the credit side.

323 D

	Dr	Cr
	$	$
Sales		258,542
Opening inventory	9,649	
Purchases	142,958	
Expenses	34,835	
Non-current assets at NBV	63,960	
Receivables	31,746	
Payables		13,864
Cash at bank	1,783	
Capital		12,525
	_____	_____
	$284,931	$284,931
	_____	_____

324 D

325 C

Both entries for the transaction (debit stationery, credit trade payables) are understated by $90, therefore the correcting entry will increase both the debit and credit totals by $90.

326 A

327 $900

Tutorial note

Correction of the second error does not involve entry to the suspense account. A credit to the payables account of twice the amount of the invoice is required to correct the first error. The corresponding debit entry is $450 to the suspense account, so increasing the balance to $900 Dr.

328 C

Tutorial note

The individual customers' accounts are not part of the general ledger.

329 A

The profit will be reduced by $250 to $24,702 by the inclusion of the invoice in expenses. As profit is reduced, the capital balance will also be reduced by $250 (to $75,591).

330 B

331 D

Suspense account opened with an entry of		$1,000 credit
Correct entry for invoice is	$1,500 debit	
Entry made was	$500 credit	
Correcting entry in property repairs account	$2,000 debit	
Entry required in suspense account		$2,000 credit
Revised balance on suspense account		$3,000 credit

332 D

333 B

334 B

For the statement of profit or loss, the total of the credit column exceeds the total of the debit column by $22,689. This represents the profit.

FINAL ACCOUNTS

335 $93,582

The opening balance is $2,304 more than the closing balance. Thus the purchases are $2,304 less than the payments, i.e. $93,582.

Tutorial note

It may be easier to consider this as a T account. Do use workings to answer multiple choice questions where necessary.

Trade payables

		B/f	13,856
Cash paid	95,886	Purchases (balancing figure)	93,582
C/f	11,552		

336 $98,995

Sales represent 125% of the cost of sales

Thus cost of sales = $120,600 × 100/125 = $96,480

Inventory value increased by $2,515

Thus purchases were $96,480 + $2,515 = $98,995

337 D

Invoice to 30 September $462 for three months, thus charge is $154 per month.

Accounts to 30 November, thus two months accrued = $308.

Charge = $1,540 + $308 = $1,848

338 C

The capital amount is paid at the end of the loan term – it is a non-current liability. Interest is incurred on a 'day-by-day' basis and, at the reporting date, no unpaid liability for interest has been incurred.

339 A

Allowance required	$2,757
Existing allowance	$2,492
Increase, therefore charge	$265

340 B

Receivables' balance ($137,850) less revised allowance ($2,757) = $135,093.

341 D

If revenue expenditure is incorrectly classified as capital expenditure, both the net profit and the net assets will be overstated. Net profit is overstated as only depreciation is deducted rather than the full cost of the expense. Net assets are overstated because revenue expenditure has been incorrectly included.

342 A

The cost of inventory includes carriage inwards (carriage outwards is charged to selling and distribution expenses). Irrecoverable debts written off are not part of cost of sales: irrecoverable debts are normally classified as administration expenses.

343

	Current asset	Non-current asset
Assets which will be converted into cash as part of normal business activity		
Assets which are used to increase productive capacity of the business		

Current assets, such as inventories or trade receivables, are normally converted into cash within 12 months.

344 B

Current		$
Payments due:	1 November 20X5	3,000
	1 May 20X6	3,000
		———
		6,000
Long term:	balance	21,000
		———
Total		27,000
		———

345 B

The provision has decreased by $500.

346 C

347 A

The trade receivables balance net of any allowance is reported as a current asset.

348 C

349 A

350 B

351 C

352 $280

Contras are the balancing figure in the receivables' ledger control account after all other figures have been entered in the account.

Receivables' ledger control account

	$		$
Balance b/d	800	Bank	6,730
Sales	6,800	Irrecoverable debts	40
		Payables contras	280
		Balance c/d	550
	7,600		7,600
Balance b/d	550		

353 C

	$
Cash owed by customers at the year end	1,300
Cash from clients during the year	28,000
	29,300
Cash owed by customers at the start of the year	(800)
Therefore sales in the year	28,500

354 A

	$
Cash owed to suppliers at the year end	200
Payments to suppliers during the year	1,800
	2,000
Payables at the start of the year	(70)
Therefore purchases in the year	1,930

355 B

	Carrying amount		Depreciation
	$		$
Furniture		(25% of 800)	200
Computer	1,575	(× 25%)	394
Printer	844	(× 25%)	211
			805

356 A

	Cost	Accumulated dep'n	Carrying amount
	$	$	$
Furniture	800	400	400
Computer	2,800	1,619	1,181
Printer	1,500	867	633
	5,100	2,886	2,214
Inventories		900	
Receivables		1,300	
Bank (see note)		3,900	
		6,100	
Payables		(200)	5,900
			8,114
Bank loans (2,400 + 2,000)			(4,400)
Net assets = Capital			3,714

Receipts = 30,000. Payments = 26,800. Cash at start of year = $700. Therefore cash at year end = 700 + 30,000 – 26,800 = 3,900.

357 B

	$
Capital at end of year	3,714
Capital at start of year	2,599
Increase in capital	1,115
Less new capital introduced	0
Add back: Drawings	24,000
Profit for the year	25,115

358 $5,450

	%	$	
Sales	220	11,000	($5,000 × 220/100)
Cost of goods sold	100	5,000	(50% × $10,000)
Gross profit	120	6,000	

	$
Gross profit	6,000
Less: Commission (5% × $11,000)	(550)
Net profit	5,450

359 A

The figure for sales can be calculated by setting up a workings account for receivables, and calculating credit sales as the balancing figure. Having calculated credit sales, total sales then equals credit sales plus cash sales.

It is assumed here that refunds to credit customers are refunds for overpayments.

Receivables (Workings account)

	$		$
Balance b/d	29,100	Cash from customers	381,600
		Expenses paid with cash from receivables	6,800
Refunds to customers	2,100	Irrecoverable debts	7,200
Sales (credit sales)	**412,400**	Contra with payables	9,400
		Balance c/d	38,600
	443,600		443,600

Total sales = Credit sales + Cash sales = $412,400 + $112,900 = $525,300.

360 B

	$
Money banked	50,000
Money from sale of car	(5,000)
Money banked from sales	45,000
Wages paid in cash	12,000
Drawings in cash	2,000
Increase in cash in till in the month	100
Sales (all cash)	59,100

361 $18,950

	$
Sales	230,000
Money banked (160,000 + 50,000)	210,000
	20,000
Increase in receivables (3,000 – 2,000)	(1,000)
Increase in cash in till (100 – 50)	(50)
Money unaccounted for = stolen	18,950

362 D

Gross profit margin = $800 = 33.33% of sales.

Sales = $800/0.3333 = $2,400.

Net profit = Gross profit – Expenses = $800 – $680 = $120.

Net profit percentage = Net profit/Sales = ($120/$2,400) × 100% = 0.05 or 5%.

363 $183,279

	$	
Opening payables	28,754	
Add purchases during the year	183,279	*Balancing figure*
Less payments during the year	(185,844)	
Closing payables	26,189	

364 $14,790

		$
Opening inventory		15,740
Add purchases during the year		75,550
Less COST of goods sold during the year	$100/120$ × $91,800	(76,500)
Closing inventory		14,790

365 $137,900

Sales = 130% of cost, thus cost of sales = $140,000

Inventory decrease of $2,100 means that purchases were $137,900.

366 $1,000

367 **$129,935**

Purchases were	payments made plus increase in suppliers' balances			
	i.e. $127,569 + ($12,826 – $11,564)		=	$128,831
Thus cost of sales	Opening inventory	$5,288		
	Purchases	$128,831		
		─────		
		$134,119		
	– Closing inventory	$4,184	=	$129,935

368 **B**

369 **B**

370 **D**

371 **A**

372 **$104,902**

Tutorial note

It may be useful to consider this as a T account. Remember to include the discounts received and the contra with the receivables control account. Do use workings to answer multiple choice questions where necessary.

Trade payables

		B/f	24,786
Cash paid	104,886	Purchases (balancing figure)	104,902
Contra with receivables	500		
Discount received	750		
C/f	23,552		
	─────		─────
	129,688		129,688
	─────		─────

373 **D**

	%	$
Sales revenue	120	240,600
Cost of sales	100	200,500
	──	─────
Gross profit	20	40,100
	──	─────

Need to adjust cost of sales for opening and closing inventory for the cost of purchases.

Purchases = $200,500 + $17,855 – $13,340 = $205,015.

374 $105,946

Tutorial note

It may be useful to consider this as a T account. Remember to include the irrecoverable debts and contra should be on the credit side of the receivables control account as they are offset against sales made in the year. Do use workings to answer multiple choice questions where necessary.

Trade receivables

Balance b/f	30,468	Cash received	105,382
Sales (balancing figure)	105,946	Contra with payables	1,000
		Irrecoverable debts	2,500
		Balance c/f	27,532
	———		———
	136,414		136,414
	———		———

375 A

Tutorial note

It may be useful to consider this as a T account. Remember to include the irrecoverable debt and the contras with the trade payables control account.

Trade receivables

Balance b/f	22,785	Cash received	95,723
Sales (balancing figure)	101,718	Contras with payables	3,750
		Amount written off	350
		Balance c/f	24,680
	———		———
	124,503		124,503
	———		———

376 B

Tutorial note

It may be useful to consider this as a T account. Remember that if an amount has already been written off as irrecoverable, it must be removed from the receivables control account. Discounts received relate to early settlement of amounts due to trade payables and is not relevant in this situation.

Trade receivables ledger control account

Balance b/f	32,785	Cash received	87,654
Sales (balancing figure)	87,312	Contra with payables	2,193
		Amount written off	127
		Balance c/f	30,123
	120,097		120,097

377 C

Tutorial note

Remember to separate the proceeds from the disposal of the asset as this is not a sales receipt – it will be used to calculate the profit or loss on disposal of that asset.

Cash account

Balance b/f	250	Banking	34,200
Cash sales (balancing figure)	36,050	Wages	3,500
Asset disposal proceeds	3,250	Drawings	1,500
		Balance c/f	350
	39,550		39,550

378 D

Cash account

Balance b/f	70	Banking	87,654
Cash sales (balancing figure)	88,959	Wages	8,750
Capital introduced	10,000	Drawings	1,825
		Laptop purchased	750
		Balance c/f	50
	99,029		99,029

379 A

Cash account

Balance b/f	100	Banking	67,890
Cash sales (balancing figure)	79,418	Wages	6,750
		Drawings	500
		Repair	350
		Purchases	3,728
		Returned goods refund	100
		Balance c/f	200
	_____		_____
	79,518		79,518
	_____		_____

To arrive at the sales figure for the month, remember to deduct the refund from the total of sales receipts: $79,418 – $100 = $79,318.

380 C

381 C

382 $33,773

Cash account

Balance b/f	70	Banking	26,543
Cash sales (balancing figure)	33,773	Wages	3,750
		Drawings	1,750
		Furniture	1,750
		Balance c/f	50
	_____		_____
	33,843		33,843
	_____		_____

383 $661,900

Cost of sales = $825,000 × 100/125 = $660,000. To word back to the purchases cost, adjust cost of sales for opening and closing inventory value = $660,000 - $12,800 + $14,700 = $661,900.

384 $125,103

Trade payables

Payments made	123,456	Balance b/f	21,876
Discount received	1,025	Purchases (balancing figure)	125,103
Contra with receivables	2,500		
Balance c/f	19,998		
	_____		_____
	146,979		146,979
	_____		_____

PARTNERSHIPS

385 B

There may be more than three persons in a partnership. Employees of a business cannot also be a partner in that business.

386 C

There is no legal requirement to have a partnership agreement; the Partnership Act will apply otherwise. It is normally an agreement confidential to the partners and set out many points on which the partners have agreed to carry on their business activities.

387 D

This would not be included within the partnership agreement, although items A, B and C would be included in the agreement.

388 C

	$	
Profit	27,800	
Less Salary – Robert	3,800	
Residual profit	24,000	
of which Vivienne's share is 3/5 or		$14,400

389 C

390 $4,800

Albert's share of the profit is calculated after deducting David's salary:
($16,000 – $8,000) × 3/5 = $4,800.

391 $24,250

	$	
Balance at 1 November 20X5	24,800	credit
Salary	6,500	credit
Interest on drawings	1,800	debit
Share of profit	12,750	credit
Drawings	18,000	debit
Balance at 31 October 20X6	24,250	credit

392 $430,000

$75,000 + $290,000 – $105,000 + $170,000 = $430,000

393 $52,750

($170,000 – (75,000 × 5%) – 8,000) = $158,250/3 = $52,750

394 $61,500

($15,000 × 5%) + 8,000 + $52,750 = $61,500

395 $9,548

Profit $30,709, less salary $14,000, thus available for appropriation = $16,709

Sam's share is 4/7 of this amount or $9,548.

396 A

	Total $	Hilda $	Stan $
Profit for the year	73,540		
Salary to Hilda	(18,000)	18,000	
	55,540		
Profit share 2:3 × $59,540	(59,540)	22,216	33,324
		40,216	33,324

397 B

	Total $	Wilma $	Jane $
Profit for the year	24,680		
Salary to Jane	(5,000)		5,000
	19,680		
Profit share 60:40 × $19,680	(19,680)	11,808	7,872
		11,808	12,872

398 $15,870

	Total $	Paul $	Linda $
Profit for the year	52,900		
Salary to Paul and Linda	(20,000)	14,000	6,000
	32,900		
Profit share 7:3 × $32,900	(32,900)	23,030	9,870
		37,030	15,870

399 D

	Total $	Sarah $	Geoff $
Profit for the year	36,600		
Salary to Geoff	(12,500)		12,500
	24,100		
Profit share 90:10 × $24,100	(32,900)	21,690	2,410
		21,690	14,910

400 B

Current accounts		Tommy	Angela
	$	$	$
Balance b/f		21,735	14,876
Drawings		(27,500)	(26,500)
Profit for year	60,000		
Salary to Tommy	(5,000)	5,000	
	55,000		
Profit share 3:5 × $55,000	(59,000)	20,625	34,375
		19,860	22,751

401 $9,094

Current accounts		Kieran	Alison
	$	$	$
Balance b/f		14,769	13,748
Drawings		(38,775)	(43,915)
Profit for year	80,000		
Salary to Kieran and Alison	(6,000)	3,500	2,500
	74,000		
Profit share 2:3 × $75,000	(74,000)	29,600	44,400
		9,094	11,733

402 A

Owners' equity

	$
Capital balances	50,000
Current balance b/f	20,625
Drawings	(34,500)
Profit for the year	150,000
	186,125

403 B

Residual profit share

	$
Profit for the year	150,000
Interest on capital (5% × $50,000)	(2,500)
Andy – salary	(12,500)
	————
Residual profit to share equally	135,000
	————
Residual profit share per partner	45,000
	————

404 C

Andy – total profit share

	$
Interest on capital (5% × $20,000)	1,000
Andy – salary	12,500
Share of profit	45,000
	————
	58,500
	————

405 D

Alan – current account balance

	$
Balance b/f	7,000
Interest on capital (5% × $20,000)	1,000
Share of profit	45,000
Drawings	(13,750)
	————
	39,250
	————

406 A

Total current account balance

	$
Total current account balances b/f	20,625
Total profit for the year	150,000
Total drawings for the year	(34,500)
	————
	136,125
	————

407 A

Residual profit share

	$
Profit for the year	45,000
Interest on capital (10% × $120,000)	(12,000)
Partnership salaries	(30,000)
Residual profit to share equally	3,000
Residual profit share per partner	1,000

Tutorial note

Note that interest on capital and partners' salaries are accounted for first as normal, and then any residual loss is dealt with in the profit sharing ratio between the partners.

408 D

	$
Interest on capital (10% × $50,000)	5,000
Partnership salary	8,000
Share of residual profit	1,000
	14,000

409

	Business expense	Profit appropriation
Salary paid to an employee	Correct	
Salary paid to a partner		Correct

'Salaries' paid to partners are an appropriation of profits, not an expense. Salary paid to an employee is a business expense.

410 A

Items B, C and D would normally be accounted for in the current account of each partner.

411 B

Accounting for goodwill on retirement of a partner is accounted for in the capital account.

412 D

$80,000 + $121,000 − $71,000 + $180,000 = $310,000

413 B

($180,000 − (80,000 × 4%) − 7,500) = $169,300 × 40% = $67,720

414 C

($28,000 × 4%) + 7,500 + ($169,300 × 40%) = $76,340

415 C

Goodwill is credited to the old partnership Gordon and Delia − $30,000 each. Goodwill is debited to the new partnership in the new profit-sharing ratio = $20,000 to each partner. This gives a debit balance of $20,000 on Mary's capital account. To clear this and have a credit balance of $10,000, she must contribute $30,000 upon joining the partnership.

416 B

Alan retirement − total amount due

	$
Capital balance b/f	60,000
Current balance b/f	15,000
Share of goodwill (1/3 × $60,000)	20,000
	95,000

417 C

Goodwill is credited to the old partnership in the profit-sharing ratio $:2. This will amount to $50,000 to John and $25,000 to Terry. Goodwill is debited to the new partnership in the new profit-sharing ratio: $25,000 for each partner. This gives a debit balance of $25,000 on Eric's capital account. To clear this and have a credit balance of $5,000, he must contribute $30,000 upon joining the partnership.

418 D

Victoria retirement − total amount due

	$
Capital balance b/f	25,000
Current balance b/f	5,000
Share of goodwill (1/3 × $90,000)	30,000
	60,000

419 A

Goodwill is initially recognised as an asset, with the corresponding credit entries made in the capital accounts of each of the 'old' partners.

420

	Debit	Credit
Partners' capital accounts	Correct	
Goodwill		Correct

Section 5

SPECIMEN EXAM QUESTIONS

Section A – ALL 50 questions are compulsory and MUST be attempted

Each question is worth 2 marks.

1   Sybil's financial year ended on 30 November 20X2. She incurred the same telephone expense each month. The last invoice paid for telephone calls was $1,800. This invoice covered the three months to 31 October 20X2.

   What adjustment is required in respect of telephone expenses when preparing the accounts to 30 November 20X2?

   A   An accrual of $1,200

   B   A prepayment of $1,200

   C   A prepayment of $600

   D   An accrual of $600

2   A trial balance fails to agree by $1,000.

   Which of the following errors could have caused the difference?

   A   A non-current asset costing $500 had been credited to the purchases account

   B   A $1,000 cheque received from a customer, F Bloggs, has been credited to J Bloggs' account in the payables ledger

   C   A rent payment of $500 had been debited to a non-current asset account

   D   A $1,000 cheque paid to a supplier had been credited to the supplier's account in the payables ledger

3   Norman is entering information into the non-current asset register.

   Which TWO information items will be used when carrying out a verification of the physical presence of non-current assets?

	Selected answer
Supplier	
Location	✓
Description	✓
Cost	

4   John has been asked to provide a copy of his final accounts to his bank manager

What is the bank manager MOST likely to use the final accounts for?

A   To calculate the tax payable on John's business profit

B   To ensure that the profit is sufficient to provide a good income for John

C   To ensure that the business is able to make the repayments on a loan

D   To ensure that John's profit margin is as good as the margin earned by other bank customers

5   Harriet is carrying out a reconciliation of her payables ledger.

Will each of the following errors lead to an entry in the general ledger control account?

	Yes	No
A payment to Bennett Dawson has been posted to the account of Dawson Bennett		✓
An invoice for $435 has been entered in the purchase day book as $345	✓	

6   **Which of the following statements correctly describes the dual aspect convention of accounting?**

A   A change in the value of assets leads to an equal change in the value of liabilities plus capital

B   Only two ledger accounts will be needed to record any transaction

C   If a transaction requires two debit entries, two credit entries must also be made

D   Transactions are recorded in both a book of prime entry and the general ledger

7   Janet valued her inventory at 30 June at its cost of $22,960. This includes some items which cost $1,950 which have been difficult to sell. Janet intends to have these items repacked at a cost of $400. She can then sell them for $900.

What will be the value of closing inventory in Janet's accounts at 30 June?

$ 21,510

8   A business has cash of $1,100, trade payables of $2,500, a mortgage liability of $8,000 and land of $16,000.

What is the capital balance?

A $10,500

B $20,400

C $6,600

D $16,000

9   Adele runs a restaurant. In August 20X3 she received a letter from a lawyer representing a customer who claims he suffered food poisoning after eating in the restaurant. The customer is claiming damages of $3,000. Adele offered to pay $300. Her lawyer's advice is that in the event of the case going to court, she is likely to be required to pay $1,500. The solicitor also advised that the court case is unlikely to take place before April 20X4.

What amount should be provided for in respect of the claim in Adele's final accounts for the year ended 30 September 20X3?

A $1,500

B $nil

C $300

D $3,000

10   Ruth started trading a year ago. She sells her products at a mark-up of 30%. In the first year of trading, she bought goods for $25,800. Her sales in the year were $30,888.

What is the value of Ruth's closing inventory?

$  2040

11   Arthur has found that an invoice for $780 for motor expenses has been posted to the correct side of the motor expenses account but the entry was made for $870.

What entry is needed to correct this error?

A   Dr Motor expenses $90   Cr Suspense $90

B   Dr Suspense $90   Cr Motor expenses $90

C   Dr Trade payables $90   Cr Suspense $90

D   Dr Suspense $90   Cr Trade payables $90

12   Ari is registered for sales tax and he has purchased goods for resale. The invoice shows the cost of the goods as $357·50, which includes sales tax at 10%.

What debit entry should be made in the purchases account?

A $357.50

B $393.25

C $325.00

D $321.75

13   At 1 September 20X1 the balance on Hai's capital account was $31,754. In the year to 31 August 20X2 he invested an additional amount of $40,000 of personal funds and took a loan of $80,000 for the business. The statement of profit or loss for the year to 31 August 20X2 reported a profit of $48,634 and Hai's drawings during the year were $28,500.

What is the closing balance on Hai's capital balance at 31 August 20X2?

$ 91 888

14   When Frank prepared his year end accounts, he made a calculation error and overstated the value of his closing inventory.

What is the effect of this error on the profit for the year and the net assets at the year end?

	Understated	*Overstated*
Profit for the year		✓
Net assets at year end		✓

15   John needs to adjust his draft year-end accounts to record a prepayment if $1,500 and an accrual of $400,

How will John's profit and net assets be affected by including the prepayment and the accrual?

A   Net profit will increase by $1,100   Net assets will reduce by $1,100

B   Net profit will reduce by $1,900   Net assets will reduce by $1,900

C   Net profit will increase by $1,100   Net assets will increase by $1,100

D   Net profit will reduce by $1,900   Net assets will increase by $1,900

16   One of Brian's customers returned goods valued at $670. The goods had been sold on credit.

What double entry should Brian post to record the return of the goods?

A   Dr Receivables' ledger control $670   Cr Sales returns $670

B   Dr Sales returns $670   Cr Receivables' ledger control $670

C   Dr Bank $670   Cr Receivables' ledger control $670

D   Dr Receivables' ledger control $670   Cr Bank $670

17   Michael and Donald have been in partnership for several years, sharing profits and losses in the ratio 3:4. At 1 January 20X4 the business had the following credit balances on the partners' capital and current accounts:

	Capital $	Current $
Michael	65,000	11,486
Donald	80,000	9,637

The partnership statement of profit or loss for the year to 31 December 20X4 disclosed a net profit of $28,595, and the partners made drawings of $16,500 each.

What is the balance brought down on Michael's current account at 31 December?

$ _____

18 At 1 October 20X1, Bakari's bank overdraft was $3,270. During the year to 30 September 20X2, he issued cheques with a total value of $189,642. His total lodgements during the year were $191,729. In addition, bank charges of $827 were incurred.

What is Bakari's bank balance brought forward at 1 October 20X2 as per his accounting records?

A $2,010 credit

B $356 credit

C $4,530 debit

D $6,184 debit

19 At 31 October the balance on the payables' control account in Tim's general ledger is $79,850 and the total of the list of balances on the personal accounts is $79,310. Tim has discovered that the difference is because a payment for $60 was entered correctly in the day book but was recorded as $600 on the supplier's account.

What is the correct value of creditors to be reported on Tim's statement of financial position at 31 October?

$ 79 850

20 Which TWO of the following errors will be revealed by extracting a trial balance?

	Selected answer
Error of single entry	✓
Error of commission	
Error of complete omission	
Error of transposition	✓

21 Which of the following is a reason for producing a trial balance?

A   To check that depreciation has been calculated correctly

B   To confirm that the balance on each ledger account has been calculated correctly

C   To check if certain errors have been made when recording transactions

D   To ensure that all transactions have been recorded

22 At 1 January 20X3 Wasan had 250 units of inventory. These were valued at $155 each. During January, the purchases and sales of the item were:

Date	Purchases	Sales
5 January		175 units
10 January	140 units at $158 per unit	
17 January		130 units
22 January	110 units at $160 per unit	
28 January		105 units

Wasan values inventory on the periodic weighted average basis.

What is the value of Wasan's inventory at 31 January 20X3 (to the nearest $1)?

A $14,400

B $14,190

C $14,125

D $14,299

23 Margaret compared her bank statement with the bank account in her general ledger and found the balances did not agree. She found two possible causes for the difference.

Do these reasons for the difference require an entry in the bank account in the general ledger?

	Yes	No
Some cheques have not been lodged by her suppliers		✓
The bank debited fees on her account	✓	

24 Alex and Jose are in partnership. Under the terms of the partnership, Alex is entitled to a salary of $11,000 per annum. In the year to 31 December 20X1, the net profit of the partnership was $43,877. Interest on capital and interest on drawings for the year have been calculated as:

	Alex	Jose
Interest on capital	$8,000	$9,500
Interest on drawings	$3,500	$5,400

What was the residual profit for the year ended 31 December 20X1?

$ 6477

25   **Which of the following statements regarding inventory valuation is correct?**

A   Inventory should be valued at anticipated selling price less any cost which will be incurred

B   All items held in inventory should be valued at cost

C   Inventory valuation should exclude profit which has not yet been earned

D   The purchase price of items which have been held for the longest period is an acceptable method for valuing inventory

26   **What is the purpose of charging depreciation?**

A   To allocate the cost of a non-current asset over the accounting periods expected to benefit from its use

B   To ensure that funds are available for the eventual replacement of the non-current asset

C   To reflect the fair value of an asset in the statement of financial position

D   To reflect the falling realisable value of an asset

27   Samantha has prepared the following bank reconciliation statement at 31 March:

	$
Balance on bank statement	1,250 (overdrawn)
Outstanding cheques	748
Outstanding lodgement	2,200
Balance on ledger account	202 (debit)

How should the bank balance be reported in Samantha's statement of financial position as at 31 March?

A $1,250 as a current liability

B $1,250 as a current asset

C $202 as a current liability

D $202 as a current asset

28   At the start of the year, the balance on Toni's capital account was $35,869. During the year Toni made drawings of $17,800 and the net profit for the year was $18,700.

What is the balance on Toni's capital account at the end of the year?

$ 36 769

29 At 30 November, Charles is owed a total of $72,660 by his customers. His receivables allowance brought forward from the previous year end was $11,700. He estimated that his receivables allowance should be equivalent to 15% of the amounts due from customers.

What amount should be included in the statement of profit or loss for the receivables expense for the year to 30 November?

A $801 debit

B $10,899 debit

C $801 credit

D $10,899 credit

30 Sarah's bank ledger control account at 30 April shows a balance at the bank of $2,280. Comparison with the bank statement at the same date reveals the following differences:

	$
Unpresented cheques	780
Bank charges not in cash book	40
Receipts not yet credited by the bank	450
Dishonoured cheques not in cash book	120

What is the correct bank ledger control account balance at 30 April?

A $1,340

B $1,950

C $2,120

D $2,360

31 Maura and Carrie have been in partnership sharing profits and losses equally. At 1 March 20X1 the total value of their capital and current balances was $225,000. At that date Delia was admitted to the partnership and it was agreed that:

(1)   The partners would share profits and losses equally

(2)   Goodwill in the business would be valued at $75,000

(3)   Goodwill would not be maintained in the books of the partnership

(4)   Delia would introduce cash to ensure that her opening capital balance is nil

How much cash must Delia contribute?

A $75,000

B $25,000

C $37,500

D $12,500

32   How should discounts which are received from suppliers for early settlement be accounted for when the statement of profit or loss is prepared?

A   As an expense included in cost of sales

B   As a deduction from the value of sales

C   As a deduction from the value of discount received

D   As an expense deducted from gross profit

33   Jessie's trial balance at 30 September 20X0 included:

	Debit $	Credit $
Receivables' ledger control account	90,350	
Allowance for irrecoverable debts brought forward		2,490

The following information is also available:

(1)   No entries have been made in respect of cash of $1,320 received from Jeffrey whose balance had been written off in the previous accounting year, and

(2)   At 30 September 20X0 an irrecoverable balance of $1,950 is to be written off and the receivable allowance is to be adjusted to 1·5% of the remaining balance

What figure will be reported in the statement of financial position at 30 September for receivables?

$ 87 080

34   **Which of the following is the reason for carrying out payables' ledger reconciliation?**

A   To check that the balance on a supplier's ledger account agrees with the supplier's statement

B   To check that the entries have been made correctly in the customer's personal accounts

C   To check that the value of purchases is correctly recorded in the general ledger

D   To check that the balance on the general ledger control account is correct

35   Alan purchased a machine on 1 March 20X1 for $12,000. He incurred additional costs for transportation of $1,300 and installation of $2,000. Shortly after he started to use the machine, it broke down and the repairs of the machine cost $600. Alan charges depreciation at 10% per annum on straight line basis with a full year's charge in the year of acquisition.

What was the correct net book value of the machine at 31 December 20X1?

$ 13 770

36 Luis and David are in partnership sharing profits and losses in the ratio 3:2. David is entitled to a salary of $9,000 and interest on capital is paid at a rate of 8% per annum. The partners' capital balances are:

Luis $75,000
David $60,000

The partnership statement of profit or loss for the year shows a profit of $58,500.

How much of the total profit is Luis entitled to?

$ 29220

37 **Which of the following correctly states the accounting equation?**

A Assets plus capital equals liabilities

B Capital plus liabilities equals assets

C Assets plus liabilities equals capital

D Capital minus liabilities equals assets

38 Fred purchased a new van. The new van cost $9,000 and Fred paid a cheque for $2,500 to the dealer. In addition the dealer accepted an old van in part exchange. The old van had been bought three years ago for $11,600 and had been depreciated by $6,750.

What is the profit or loss on disposal of the old van?

A $1,650 profit

B $6,500 profit

C $1,650 loss

D $6,500 loss

39 Lance is entering an invoice with the following details into the purchase day book. The invoice shows the following costs:

	$
Water treatment equipment	39,800
Delivery	1,100
Maintenance charge	3,980
Sales tax	7,854
Invoice total	52,734

What is the total value of capital expenditure on the invoice?

A $52,734

B $44,880

C $39,800

D $40,900

40   Lorna is preparing her monthly receivables' ledger reconciliation. She has discovered that a credit balance of $79 on a customer's account has been treated as a debit balance.

To complete the reconciliation, what adjustment should Lorna make to the total of the list of balances?

A   Reduce the total by $158

B   Increase the total by $79

C   Reduce the total by $79

D   Increase the total by $158

41   Nandita has bought goods for resale on credit from Pascale. The goods cost $600 before sales tax, which is calculated at 10%.

When the transaction is posted to the general ledger, which TWO of the following entries should be included?

	Selected answer
Cr Purchase ledger control account	✓
Dr Purchases	✓
Cr Sales tax	
Cr Bank	

42   At 30 September 20X3 Pamela's inventory was valued at $6,400 and her trial balance included the following balances:

	Debit $	Credit $
Sales		45,000
Purchases	29,500	
Inventory at 1 October 20X2	5,700	
Carriage inwards	750	
Postage	340	
Wages	6,000	
Advertising	1,900	
Other expenses	2,500	

What was Pamela's gross profit for the year ended 30 September 20X3?

A $4,710

B $15,110

C $15,450

D $16,200

43 **If an extended trial balance had been completed and the result was a loss, into which columns would the result be entered?**

A   Statement of profit or loss – Debit   Statement of financial position - Debit

B)   Statement of profit or loss – Credit   Statement of financial position - Debit

C   Statement of profit or loss – Credit   Statement of financial position - Credit

D   Statement of profit or loss – Debit   Statement of financial position - Credit

44 Consider the following statements about going concern:

(1)   Financial statements must always be prepared on the going concern basis

(2)   If a business is not considered to be a going concern, financial statements should not be prepared.

Which of the statements is/are correct?

A   2 only

B   1 only

C   Both 1 and 2

D)   Neither 1 nor 2

45 At 30 November 20X3, Zoltan's bank current account was overdrawn. He also had a bank loan on which monthly capital repayments will commence in February 20X5.

How should these balances be reported on his statement of financial position at 30 November 20X3?

	Current asset	Current liability	Non-current liability
Bank Loan			✓
Bank current account		✓	

46 James has been advised that one of his customers has ceased trading and that he will not recover the balance of $720 owed by his customer.

What entry should James make in his general ledger?

A   Dr Receivables;' ledger control $720   Cr Receivables expense $720

B)   Dr Receivables expense $720   Cr Receivables' ledger control $720

C   Dr Receivables' ledger control $720   Cr Bank $720

D   Dr Bank $720   Cr Receivables' ledger control $720

47   When the extended trial balance is being completed, in which column should the value for a bank overdraft be entered?

A   Statement of profit or loss credit

B   Statement of financial position credit

C   Statement of financial position debit

D   Statement of profit or loss debit

48   The amount owed to Jane by her customers at 31 October was $34,729. A year earlier she was owed $27,641. During the year Jane had lodged $327,684 to her bank account. This included payments received from her customers as well as $45,000 which Jane had received from the sale of her holiday home.

What was the value of Jane's sales for the year ended 31 October?

A $289,772

B $334,772

C $327,684

D $282,684

49   Assume that the extended trial balance has been extended but the result for the year has not yet been calculated. The totals of the statement of profit or loss and the statement of financial position columns are:

Statement of profit or loss   Statement of financial position

Dr $473,954   Cr $485,889   Dr $172,544   Cr $160,609

Which of the following is the correct result for the year?

A   A profit of $11,944

B   A loss of $11,944

C   A profit of $11,935

D   A loss of $11,935

50   Which accounting principle is applied when two similar transactions are treated in the same way?

A   Materiality

B   Consistency

C   Accruals

D   Double entry

(Total: 100 marks)

Section 6

ANSWERS TO SPECIMEN EXAM QUESTIONS

1   D

November 20X2 telephone payment is accrued.

Payment for November 20X2 = $1800 ÷ 3 = $600

2   A

3

	Selected answer
Supplier	
Location	Correct
Description	Correct
Cost	

4   C

5

	Yes	No
A payment to Bennett Dawson has been posted to the account of Dawson Bennett		Correct
An invoice for $435 has been entered in the purchase day book as $345	Correct	

6   A

7 $21,510

$22,960 – $1,950 + ($900 – $400) = $22,510

8   C

$16,000 + $1,100 – $2,500 – $8,000 = $6,600

9   A

10 $2,040

$25,800 – ($30,888/1.3) = $2,040

11   B

12   C

$357.50/ (1 + 0.10) = $325.00

13 $91,888

Bal b/f $31,754 + Cap Intro $40,000 + Profit $48,634 – Drawings $28,500 = $91,888

14

	Understated	*Overstated*
Profit for the year		Correct
Net assets at year end		Correct

15   C

16   B

17 $7,241 CREDIT

Bal b/f $11,486 + Profit share $12,255 – Drawings $16,500 = $7,241 credit

18   A

Bank o/d b/f ($3,270) – chqs issued $189,642 + lodgements $191,729 – bank charges $827 = $2,010 overdrawn i.e. credit balance

19 $79,850

20

	Selected answer
Error of single entry	Correct
Error of commission	
Error of complete omission	
Error of transposition	Correct

21   C

22   **C**

Periodic weighted average rate:

[(250 × $155) + (140 × $158) + (110 × $160)]/(250 + 140 + 110) = $156.94

Closing inventory (units) = 250 – 175 + 140 – 130 + 110 – 105 = 90

Closing inventory (value) = $156.94 × 90 = $14,125

23

	Yes	No
Some cheques have not been lodged by her suppliers		No
The bank debited fees on her account	Yes	

24   **$24,277**

Net profit $43,877 – Salary $11,000 – Int on capital $17,500 + Int on drawings $8,900 = $24,277.

25   **C**

26   **A**

27   **D**

28   **$36,769**

Balance b/f $35,869 –- drawings $17,800 + profit $18,700 = $36,769

29   **C**

$11,700 – (15% of $72,660) = $801 credit

30   **C**

$2,280 – $40 – $120 = $2,120

31   **B**

Delia would need to introduce capital of contribute capital 1/3 of $75,000 = $25,000. Remember that goodwill is credited to the goodwill account (to remove it from the accounting records) and the "new partners' are debited in their profit-sharing ratio i.e. $25,000 is credited to the capital account of each partner. Delia must therefore introduce capital of $25,000.

32   **B**

33 **$87,074**

$90,350 – $1,950 – 1.5% of ($90,350 – $1,950) = $87,074

34 **D**

35 **$13,770**

$12,000 + $1,300 + $2,000 – 10% of ($12,000 + $1,300 + $2,000) = $13,770

36 **$29,220**

Available profit $58,500 – $9,000 – 8% of 75,000 – 8% of 60,000) = $38,700
Luis share (3/5) × $38,700 + Interest on capital = $23,220 + $6,000 = $29,220

37 **B**

38 **A**

$9,000 – ($2,500 + ($11,600 – $6,750)) = $1,650 profit

39 **D**

$39,800 + $1,100 = $40,900. Note that sales tax is not part of the capitalised cost.

40 **A**

41

	Selected answer
Cr Purchase ledger control account	Correct
Dr Purchases	Correct
Cr Sales tax	
Cr Bank	

42 **C**

$45,000 + $6,400 – ($29,500 + $5,700 + $750) = $15,450

43 **B**

44 **D**

45

	Current asset	Current liability	Non-current liability
Bank Loan			Correct
Bank current account		Correct	

46 **B**

47 **B**

48 **A**

$327,684 – $45,000 + ($34,729 – $27,641) = $289,772

49 **C**

$485,889 – $473,954 = $11,935 profit

50 **B**